THE DISCIPLINE
OF SURRENDER

BIBLICAL IMAGES
OF DISCIPLESHIP

DOUGLAS D. WEBSTER

InterVarsity Press
Downers Grove, Illinois

InterVarsity Press
P.O. Box 1400, Downers Grove, IL 60515-1426
World Wide Web: www.ivpress.com
E-mail: mail@ivpress.com

InterVarsity Press® is the book-publishing division of InterVarsity Christian Fellowship/USA®, a student
movement active on campus at hundreds of universities, colleges and schools of nursing in the United
States of America, and a member movement of the International Fellowship of Evangelical Students. For
information about local and regional activities, write Public Relations Dept., InterVarsity Christian
Fellowship/USA, 6400 Schroeder Rd., P.O. Box 7895, Madison, WI 53707-7895.

All Scripture quotations, unless otherwise indicated, are taken from the Holy Bible, New International
Version®. NIV®. Copyright ©1973, 1978, 1984 by International Bible Society. Used by permission of
Zondervan Publishing House. All rights reserved.

John Updike's Easter poem (p. 115) is reprinted from Telephone Poles and Other Poems by John
Updike. Copyright©1963 by John Updike. Reprinted by permission of Alfred A. Knopf, a division of
Random House Inc.

Other permissions pending.

Cover photograph: Michael Goss

ISBN 0-8308-2282-8

Printed in the United States of America ∞

Library of Congress Cataloging-in-Publication Data

Webster, Douglas D.
  The discipline of surrender : biblical images of discipleship / Douglas D. Webster
    p.   cm.
  Includes bibliographical references (p.).
  ISBN 0-8308-2282-8 (paper : alk. paper)
    1. Christian life—Biblical teaching.   I. Title.

BS680.C47 W43 2001
248.4—dc21
                                                                          00-047154

20 19 18 17 16 15 14 13 12 11 10 9 8 7 6 5 4 3 2 1

17 16 15 14 13 12 11 10 09 08 07 06 05 04 03 02 01

To
my mother
Louise Webster
in thanksgiving
for your
lifelong surrender
to Christ

And to
First Presbyterian Church
of San Diego
in gratitude for
your partnership
in the gospel

CONTENTS

1

Biblical Images

If anyone would come after me,
he must deny himself and take up his cross daily and follow me.
For whoever wants to save his life will lose it,
but whoever loses his life for me will save it.

LUKE 9:23-24

Now the Lord is the Spirit,
and where the Spirit of the Lord is, there is freedom.
And we, who with unveiled faces all reflect the Lord's glory,
are being transformed into his likeness with ever-increasing glory,
which comes from the Lord, who is the Spirit.

2 CORINTHIANS 3:17-18

In the spring of 1999 several Serbian leaders accused of genocidal ethnic cleansing were interviewed for a television documentary titled *Yugoslavia: The Death of a Nation.* I imagine most viewers noticed the religious icons on prominent display behind the well-dressed indicted war criminals. It was provocative to see these men associate Christianity with their sinful cause. They proudly displayed icons of saints and Christ as they calmly defended atrocities. They did not speak of Christianity, but with simple icons in the background they sought to

impress the viewer with their religious motivation. It was as if they
were using Christ's letterhead to send their message.

In a culture that is as visually oriented as ours, symbols have a
powerful impact. They leave us with impressions that often run far
deeper than we realize. Advertisers know the power of corporate
logos. It's worth millions to Nike for Tiger Woods to wear a black cap
with their white swoosh. The unfurling of the nation's flag can bring a
crowd to attention and tears to the eyes of war veterans. The Muslim
crescent, the Jewish menorah and the Christian cross symbolize three
world religions and invoke powerful feelings. A Jewish neighbor visit-
ing our home became upset when she saw a decorative plate hanging
on our kitchen wall. The hand-painted Star of David with a cross in
the center deeply disturbed her. She would have been fine if we had a
cross hanging in the kitchen, but the combination of symbols was
offensive to her.

The Bible has plenty of "visual aids" that instruct us in what it
means to fear God and follow the Lord. Like the unadorned altar or
the easy yoke they visualize the truth of God for us. The purpose of
this book is to reveal God's objects of instruction for what they are:
meaningful symbols designed by God to encourage us in the discipline of surrender. We may miss the significance of the ancient gift of
manna or of the everyday occurrence of a crowing rooster if we don't
take the time to examine them carefully. Some of these biblical images
are more obvious, such as the Lamb of God, while others, like
Gideon's trumpet, may seem obscure. But all point to the believer's
surrender to the sovereign care of God.

One of my goals is to fix in our memory these biblical images so
that whenever we see these objects we remember what they signify.
My hope is that when we grab for a towel we will think of Jesus on
bended knee washing the disciples' feet, or when we hear a trumpet
we will think of Gideon's trumpet and be reminded of our dependence on the Lord of hosts. We want to pay attention to the significance of the imagery of the farmer's yoke and of a sharp thorn. We
want to realize the spiritual significance of a clay pot and of a little

lamb and apply their messages to our lives. As a logo stands for a company, these biblical images stand for a way of life.

Some of my friends have found the Eastern Orthodox Church and its enthusiastic use of icons in worship to be very impressive. Their fascination with icons led me to seriously consider the powerful yet earthy images found in God's Word. I quickly became impressed with the power of symbols in Scripture and with God's desire to use vivid pictures to shape our response to himself. I came to the conclusion that biblical images are very different from religious icons. Biblical images serve as object lessons for instruction rather than objects of devotion. They retain their humility and earthiness and draw attention to a way of living for Christ in ordinary life. They help define the character of Christian discipleship. They appeal to our imagination in order to shape our understanding of what it means to follow Jesus.

Biblical images are typically found outside the church, in ordinary life, in the world of work and family. They are not easily transformed by artists into works of art. They resist beautification and ornamentation. Biblical images are simple, ordinary objects that are used by God to make a point. No one is ever going to take aesthetic pride in a pile of rocks or bow before a towel and basin. A farmer's yoke or a crowing rooster seems out of place in the sanctuary. Yet each of these biblical images offers a key insight into what it means to surrender our lives to Christ.

One of the most significant truths about biblical images is that their meaning is defined by the biblical text. Like symbols on a map they require an interpretive key to determine their meaning. Behind each image is a true story that shapes its meaning and guides us in how to live for God. Apart from the biblical story and the vivid experience of the text, these objects mean nothing. Donkeys and piles of rocks do not convey spiritual significance by themselves. It is only when we remember the will of God as it is symbolized in these simple object lessons that we benefit from biblical images. It is only when these images highlight a truth from salvation history that we see their incomparable value. People may bring their own special meaning to

religious icons, but biblical images have their own meaning inspired
by the Word of God. By the Holy Spirit they reflect God's strategy for
spiritual growth. These down-to-earth visual aids help us to understand what it means to humbly submit to Jesus Christ as our Lord.

The Pattern

The inner logic of how Christians grow up in the faith is well illustrated throughout the Bible. God makes his message clear. Nevertheless, it is often difficult for us to grasp the true meaning of Christian
discipleship because it contradicts the spirit of our culture and fallen
human nature. We frustrate ourselves. We feel compelled to perform
and make something of ourselves. Instead of pursuing ministry we
aspire for prominence. Instead of bowing before the name that is
above every name, we strive to make a name for ourselves. Even when
we have given up hope of ever amounting to much, we draw attention
to ourselves. We blame God. We blame others. We blame ourselves.
Instead of choosing a life of abandonment to Christ we feel abandoned. The quest for self-recognition and self-sufficiency is so strong
that even the language of surrender sounds foreign and unappealing.
We have trouble imagining what surrendering to the will of God is
like.

Our failure to get the picture often leads to artificial efforts to
jumpstart a more meaningful life in Christ. Well-intentioned advisers
invent new programs and techniques that promise renewal. Stages of
spiritual growth are plotted and a spiritual to-do list is drawn up. We
are faced with a lot of practical advice wherever we turn, but something is missing. Try as we might, we can't seem to get the picture of
soul-satisfying discipleship in focus, but the Word of God gives plenty
of encouragement to help us get our act together and take positive
initiative. Jesus' parable of the shrewd manager (Lk 16) is a good
example. You may recall that the shrewd manager was about to lose
his job because of his mismanagement, so he cleverly made friends
with his boss's clients by drastically reducing what they owed. He carried out this shrewd maneuver so that when he was fired he would

have some wealthy "friends" who owed him a favor. Although this tactic didn't help him keep his job, it did impress his boss, who commended him for his creative long-range planning. He had finally taken some initiative!

The point of the parable is that if people in the world can take initiative for dishonest gain to save their skin, we can take the initiative in following Christ for the sake of our souls. So we give ourselves a pep talk to stop making excuses and get on with the job. We eagerly look for a five- or ten-step formula for Christian success. We want a "read-my-lips" approach to discipleship that is so clear and step by step that we cannot fail.

We all know some areas in our lives where we have failed. All of us can look at our relationships, our work performance, our health and our spiritual life and see major ways we need to improve. Who wouldn't benefit from the sage advice in Proverbs? "Go to the ant, you sluggard; consider its ways and be wise! It has no commander, no overseer or ruler, yet it stores its provisions in summer and gathers its food at harvest" (Prov 6:6-8).

But taking initiative is not the starting point for spiritual growth. There is something prior to this theme that is foundational for maturity. Instead of a quest for success there needs to be a rest for the soul, from which life's meaning, purpose and significance issue. Which makes for a better life verse, "Lazy hands make a man poor, but diligent hands bring wealth" (Prov 10:4) or "Trust in the LORD with all your heart and lean not on your own understanding; in all your ways acknowledge him, and he will make your paths straight" (Prov 3:5-6)? There are plenty of verses that call us to action, such as Ecclesiastes 9:10, "Whatever your hand finds to do, do it with all your might," but the wisdom of Psalm 46:10, "Be still, and know that I am God," precedes the call to do something.

I'm suggesting that there is a kind of DNA blueprint for spiritual growth, a blueprint that is both spiritually dynamic and irreducibly complex. There is a principle or a paradigm at work in each and every experience of spiritual renewal. It is the truth that precedes the call to action and the challenge to take initiative. It is what must be received before we can achieve anything that pleases God.

Biochemist Michael Behe, in his excellent book *Darwin's Black Box*, makes a case for creation's intelligent design by exploring the irreducible complexity of a single cell. Even at this infinitesimal level of life we find systems so miraculously complex that they never could have been randomly orchestrated. Behe contends that there is actually no such thing as a simple cell. The deeper and closer we look at a cell, the more we discover the mystery of its complexity. This is true as well for our life with God. There is no such thing as a simple formula that could ever lead us to spiritual success. The deeper and closer we look, the more complex and challenging true spiritual growth is. We come to understand that at the core of life in Christ is not a formula for success but a faithfulness in brokenness. The inner logic of the Christian life is not about making something of ourselves but about allowing God to do whatever he wants with us. In other words, the DNA-like blueprint for spiritual growth is not the will to perform but the discipline of surrender. This is the foundational truth that shapes our life in Christ.

The Image

Each of the biblical images that we will explore illustrates the discipline of surrender. They will impress upon us what is involved in taking up our cross daily and following Jesus. With the help of the Holy Spirit these instruments of instruction will shape our life in Christ and help us to better understand what it means to be his disciple. The beauty of these images is that within God's salvation history they deliver a single message that symbolizes the spoken message of Jesus. They capture in simple form the dynamic of Christ-centered discipleship.

In my backyard I have two items that require no explanation: a hammock and a punching bag. You don't need me to tell you that a hammock symbolizes relaxation and a punching bag stands for a tension-relieving workout. We are surrounded by objects that convey a simple message about us. In our church we celebrate what we call Banner Sunday on All Saints Day. We remember our brothers and sisters in Christ who have died during the past year. With help from adults, children make a banner representing the life of each saint. They may cut out a felt plane for a pilot or a Bible for a Sunday school teacher or a hammer for a carpenter. They glue five or six symbols on a banner and then we hang all the banners around the sanctuary. It has proved to be a meaningful experience for the entire congregation as we remember these dear saints and our hope in the power of Christ's resurrection. Because of our activities and our commitments certain symbols represent who we are. Although they may be fairly mundane, these visual images can stir the emotions and express profound personal commitments.

The simple, earthy images in the Bible that help to capture the essence of our lives in Christ ultimately trace their significance to an image that is not a symbol but a *person*. The meaning of the biblical metaphors we will explore rests in the reality of the incarnate One. Quoting from an early Christian hymn the apostle Paul focused on this truth: "Precisely because he was in the form of God he did not consider being equal with God grounds for grasping. On the contrary, he rather poured himself out by taking the form of a slave, by being born in the likeness of human beings, and by being recognized as a man. He humbled himself, by becoming obedient even to the point of accepting death, and that of all things, death on a cross" (Phil 2:6-8).[1]

The meaning of discipleship and the significance of the biblical metaphors that illustrate discipleship are founded upon the person and work of Christ. Old Testament biblical images point forward to the reality of the coming Christ. And New Testament metaphors depend on the all-important, history-changing fact of the incarnation. "The Word became flesh and made his dwelling among us. We have seen his glory, the glory of the One and Only, who came from the Father, full of grace and truth" (Jn 1:14). This is the essential reality that gives rise to the meaning of these biblical images for discipleship. It is not metaphor based on metaphor or symbol layered on symbol but meaning derived from God incarnate, the Son who "is the radiance of God's glory and the exact representation of his being" (Heb 1:3). To declare that Jesus is the Way, the Truth and the Life is not to use mythical language to say that life is important but to use historical language to confess the Author of Life.

Biblical images illustrate the significance of Christ and his call to discipleship in ways that are both memorable and practical. Their value resides completely in the reality of Christ. When biblical images are used in sentimental or self-gratifying ways, their meaning can be diminished or lost altogether. Take the common Advent symbol of the manger. When Luke quoted the angelic announcement "This will be a sign to you: You will find a baby wrapped in cloths and lying in a manger," he introduced a powerful metaphor for God's self-imposed, sacrificial powerlessness (Lk 2:12). In this divinely appointed object lesson the manger becomes a profound illustration of the humility of God. It is a radical picture of God's self-emptying. God himself, in the man Christ Jesus, condescends to join our helpless state in order to redeem us and restore us to right relationship with himself. Like the cross, the manger illustrates the extent of Christ's love. It is easy to see from this simple visual aid that God went all the way in experiencing the fullness of our humanity, but today it may not be as easy to apply the meaning of the manger to the followers of Jesus. Do we entertain the notion that God seeks to advance the gospel through our prominence and worldly success? The message of the manger strongly implies otherwise.

Also, if we're not careful we can twist the message of Christ's manger and use it to "baby" our faith. The manger can be transposed from a symbol of surrender and humility into a seasonal symbol generating feelings of warmth and tenderness. The manger can be used nostalgically to symbolize maternal love instead of Christ's sacrifice; it can be used sentimentally to symbolize the gift of babies instead of the gift of salvation. How we invoke the biblical image of the manger determines whether we use or abuse this symbol.

If Christ and his Word shape the meaning behind the metaphor, then God's visual aids will retain their effectiveness in shaping discipleship. Our aim is to understand these biblical images in the light of God's salvation history and apply their message in a way that strengthens and inspires our faithfulness to Christ.

2

The Unadorned Altar

Then the LORD said to Moses, "Tell the Israelites this:
'You have seen for yourselves that I have spoken to you from heaven:
Do not make any gods to be alongside me;
do not make for yourselves gods of silver or gods of gold.

" 'Make an altar of earth for me and sacrifice on it your burnt offerings and
fellowship offerings, your sheep and goats and your cattle.
Wherever I cause my name to be honored, I will come to you
and bless you. If you make an altar of stones for me,
do not build it with dressed stones,
for you will defile it if you use a tool on it.
And do not go up to my altar on steps,
lest your nakedness be exposed on it.' "

EXODUS 20:22-26

An entire nation was moved by the tragedy at Texas A&M University when a fifty-five-foot tower of logs collapsed, killing twelve students. It was an Aggie tradition to light the world's largest bonfire the night before the big game with their archrival, the University of Texas. A saying often repeated in defense of the bonfire tradition went like this:

"From the outside looking in, you can't understand it, and from the inside looking out, you can't explain it." I'll let you decide whether or not that saying helps justify the Texas A&M bonfire, but it strikes me as just the opposite of what Christians should say about discipleship. God never intended to make a mystery out of obedience or a secret out of his call. What it means to follow the Lord is clearly revealed. God's object lessons of instruction are understandable to the outsider and can be simply explained by the insider.

The discipline of surrender is illustrated from the beginning of God's salvation history. It is easy to see a pattern of willed passivity in the life of Abraham. The Lord said to Abraham, "Leave your country, your people and your father's household and go to the land I will show you."

> I will make you into a great nation
>   and I will bless you;
> I will make your name great,
>   and you will be a blessing.
> I will bless those who bless you,
>   and whoever curses you I will curse;
> and all peoples on earth
>   will be blessed through you. (Gen 12:1-3)

Unlike the people of Shinar, who attempted to make a name for themselves by building the tower of Babel (Gen 11), the Lord promised to establish and bless Abraham and to make his name great.

Wherever Abraham went in that foreign land, he built an altar to the Lord and called on the name of the Lord. Of course, the most significant altar he ever built came some thirty-five years after his original call, when God told him to sacrifice his son Isaac. On that altar Abraham's faith was tested like it had never been tested before. Abraham lived by faith. His words to Isaac as they climbed Mount Moriah proved it: "God himself will provide the lamb for the burnt offering, my son" (Gen 22:8). You know the history; you've seen the pattern. Abraham is prevented from sacrificing Isaac, but the pattern is fixed in our praying imagination. God the Father will go all the way by giving his one and only Son. On Abraham's wilderness roadmap he called this place "The LORD Will Provide."

The pattern of divine initiative and human surrender is evident in the lives of Jacob and Joseph, and it is clearly at the heart of Moses' identity. Moses used every excuse he could think of, but none of them worked with God. This wilderness-wandering man without a country came face to face with his weak, insecure and defensive self. He was confronted by the living God who declared, "I AM WHO I AM." In spite of Moses' resistance and reticence God's identity and power shaped him. When Moses built an altar he called it "The LORD is my Banner" (Ex 17:15). It stood in marked contrast to the golden calf that Aaron and the Israelites later smelted and erected while Moses was on Mount Sinai. Even though Aaron dedicated this idol to the Lord and called the occasion "a festival to the LORD" (Ex 32:5), it stood for everything false. Nothing about it was true. It was a vain, religious attempt to rally the troops. The tower of Babel and the golden calf were both fashioned out of human fear and pride in self-centered efforts to please man-made gods. Idols are products of self-centered, self-pleasing fascination. Altars are reflections of self-surrendered, self-humbling faithfulness.

Wherever we look in the Bible, willed passivity is the pattern for kingdom of God effectiveness. It is the modus operandi for paring down Gideon's troops from thirty-two thousand to three hundred so that Israel would not claim "that her own strength" had saved her (Judg 7:2). It was a deeply held conviction in the life of David, even from a young age, as we clearly hear in his response to Goliath: "You come against me with sword and spear and javelin, but I come against you in the name of the LORD Almighty" (1 Sam 17:45). We cannot understand the lives of Nehemiah or Daniel apart from the principle of willed passivity.

Mary, the mother of Jesus, illustrated this principle when she said, "I am the Lord's servant. . . . May it be to me as you have said" (Lk 1:38). John the Baptist said it as succinctly as anyone when he declared about Jesus, "He must become greater; I must become less" (Jn 3:30). The apostle Paul was adamant on the subject: "If anyone

thinks he has reasons to put confidence in the flesh, I have more. . . .
But whatever was to my profit I now consider loss for the sake of
Christ. . . . I consider them rubbish, that I may gain Christ" (Phil
3:4-8). He summarized well the discipline of surrender when he
quoted the Lord's response to his "thorn in the flesh": "My grace is
sufficient for you, for my power is made perfect in weakness" (2 Cor
12:9). In exile the elderly John is a picture of willed passivity: "I,
John, your brother and companion in the suffering and kingdom
and patient endurance that are ours in Jesus, was on the island of
Patmos because of the word of God and the testimony of Jesus" (Rev
1:9).

The fullest manifestation of the discipline of surrender is evident
in our Lord and Savior, Jesus Christ. It is beautifully summarized in a
single line from Jesus' prayer to the Father: "Not my will, but yours be
done" (Lk 22:42). Is not the incarnation the greatest act of willed passivity second only to death on the cross?

> Your attitude should be the same as that of Christ Jesus:
> Who, being in very nature God,
>   did not consider equality with God something to be grasped,
> but made himself nothing,
>   taking the very nature of a servant,
>   being made in human likeness.
> And being found in appearance as a man,
>   he humbled himself
>   and became obedient to death—
>   even death on a cross! (Phil 2:4-8)

The principle of divine surrender is what Jesus lived out and what he
calls us to practice: "If anyone would come after me, he must deny
himself and take up his cross daily and follow me. For whoever wants
to save his life will lose it, but whoever loses his life for me will save
it" (Lk 9:23-24).

A Picture
In the wilderness Moses and the people of Israel were given spe-

cific instructions on how to build an altar. From the days of Abraham and even Abel before him, the altar has been a symbol of sacrifice and surrender. Noah built an altar after the flood, and Job offered burnt offerings on behalf of his family. The people of God had been building altars for centuries before they were given specific instructions on how to build them. Apparently Abraham knew how to build an altar without reading a manual. There wasn't much to it. There was no art to building an altar. It was just a pile of rocks.

The key factor in authentic God-centered worship was not the shape or size of the altar but the worshiper's humble dependence on the mercy of God. Abraham knew that, but in time the simplicity of true worship was tainted by human nature's predisposition to reverse the meaning of worship and glorify the self. Cultural influences crept in, and the children of Abraham were tempted to exalt rather than humble themselves. They could easily turn true worship into idolatry and shift attention away from the mercy of God to religious style and performance. This religious danger necessitated the following command:

> If you make an altar of stones for me, do not build it with dressed stones, for you will defile it if you use a tool on it. And do not go up to my altar on steps, lest your nakedness be exposed on it. (Ex 20:25-26)

The unadorned, undecorated pile of rocks in the wilderness became for the people a biblical image. It stood there in earthy simplicity as a symbol of human need and divine acceptance, humility and mercy, repentance and redemption. The Lord insisted that the altar must not be turned into a shrine to human effort and religious pride. To decorate the altar was to desecrate it. To put it high up on a platform was to exalt humanity and debase God. "Whatever you do," the Lord said in effect, "don't work on it religiously. Keep it simple. It's just a pile of rocks. Worship me in humility and depend on my mercy."

What this picture means in our personal lives is captured in Pastor George Herbert's poem "The Altar," first published in 1633:

A broken ALTAR, Lord thy servant rears,
Made of a heart, and cemented with tears:
Whose parts are as thy hand did frame;
No workman's tool hath touched the same.
A HEART alone
Is such a stone,
As nothing but
Thy power doth cut.
Wherefore each part
Of my hard heart
Meets in this frame,
To praise thy Name:
That, if I chance to hold my peace,
These stones to praise thee may not cease.
Oh let thy blessed SACRIFICE be mine,
And sanctify this ALTAR to be thine.

What first catches my eye is the shape of the poem. What Herbert
made of his poem is what God intends to make of our lives. It is not
we who fashion ourselves into something religious and acceptable to
God. All such willful action ends in idolatry. If we insist on control-
ling our destiny, limiting our involvement with God and being the
master of our fate, we only succeed in exposing our sinfulness. The
essence of life is not what we make of ourselves but what God makes
of us. Will you let God make something of you or will you insist on
your own master plan? When you look at this poem, you may see
either an altar or the letter *I*. For Herbert both symbols were meant to
mean the same thing. Is your identity, your *I*, in the shape of an altar?
The apostle Paul's challenge comes to mind, "I urge you, brothers, in
view of God's mercy, to offer your bodies as living sacrifices, holy and
pleasing to God–this is your spiritual act of worship" (Rom 12:1).

It is not only the shape of the poem that stands out but the number
of biblical allusions. Of course Exodus 20 was in Herbert's mind as he
reflected on the difference between an altar and an idol. "No workman's tool hath touched the same" recalls the command not to defile
an altar with our own designs. We are forever tempted to turn the
work and worship of God into a platform for our own self-expression

and self-promotion. When that happens, the altar becomes an idol. Herbert's reference to a stony heart makes us think of the hardheartedness of Israel, which resisted God's will in the wilderness. "A HEART alone / Is such a stone" leads each of us to reflect on the condition of our own heart. We know that a warm and engaging personality can conceal a heart of stone. We know that outward conformity and compliance can cover up an unyielding heart.

"As nothing but / Thy power doth cut" recalls the ways God has worked to break our stubborn, self-centered wills and to lead us to praise him. It is this hard heart of mine that now by the grace of God "meets in this frame / To praise thy Name." Drawing on the apostle Peter's analogy, we are "living stones . . . being built into a spiritual house to be a holy priesthood, offering spiritual sacrifices acceptable to God through Jesus Christ" (1 Pet 2:5). When we read "these stones to praise thee may not cease," we remember what Jesus said to the hardhearted Pharisees: "I tell you, if they [the disciples] keep quiet, the stones will cry out" (Lk 19:40).

It's not the altar that is most important, after all, but the sacrifice. "Oh let thy blessed SACRIFICE be mine, / And sanctify this ALTAR to be thine." Examine the line carefully to see if it is the expression of your heart. You may not use these metaphors, but do you accept their meaning? Divine initiative is Herbert's theme. A prayer for mercy seeks the redemption to be found in Christ's atoning sacrifice. A prayer of consecration asks the Lord to set apart our lives for his purpose. We do not sound like this today, but we should. George Herbert's poem will undoubtedly impress some as odd or quaint, but I pray that it will express for many earnest followers of Christ the longing of their hearts.

The altar is a good place to begin to understand the discipline of surrender. It reminds me of that old gospel hymn written by Charlotte Elliott in 1844, which begins, "Just as I am, without one plea / But that thy blood was shed for me." The altar symbolizes our repentance and God's mercy. It's just a pile of rocks. There must be no vain attempt to beautify the harsh realities represented in the altar. There are no grounds for religious merit. Repentance is a sacrifice laid on an altar of unadorned stones.

A quest for deeper devotion to Christ may begin in many ways. We could discuss spiritual gifts, what they are and who has which gifts; we might talk about the need for more prayer or better strategies of evangelism; we could emphasize church growth and proven techniques for effective youth work. These all may be good, but the foundational truth that precedes them is the discipline of surrender. Willed passivity is our first consideration. Are we willing for our hearts of stone to be cut by the only one who has the power to make us and shape us into his image? Are we willing to have our lives become altars made of hearts, cemented with tears? Herein lies God's plan for our spiritual renewal and growth in Christ. God's object lessons begin with an unadorned altar.

3

The Shepherd's Staff

Moses answered, "What if they do not believe me or listen to me and say,
'The LORD did not appear to you'?"
Then the LORD said to him, "What is that in your hand?"
"A staff," he replied.
The LORD said, "Throw it on the ground."
Moses threw it on the ground and it became a snake, and he ran from it.
Then the LORD said to him, "Reach out your hand and take it by the tail."
So Moses reached out and took hold of the snake and it
turned back into a staff in his hand. "This," said the LORD,
"is so that they may believe that the LORD, the God of their fathers—
the God of Abraham, the God of Isaac and the God of Jacob—
has appeared to you."

EXODUS 4:1-5

Recently I received a small icon in the mail from a friend who belongs to an Eastern Orthodox church. Today we're familiar with the term *icon* because of our computers. We click on an icon to open a program. In the Eastern Orthodox tradition an icon represents a sacred person such as Jesus or one of the apostles or a saint. Since ancient times icons of Christ and the saints have been used in worship. My three-by-five-inch replication of an ancient picture of Jesus bears the seal of approval, the imprimatur, of the Syrian Church. Not long ago I attended an Eastern Orthodox service. At the conclusion of the service the worshipers filed forward and made the sign of the cross before a picture of Jesus held in the hands of the priest. Some of them kissed the hand of the priest or kissed the icon.

God's Object Lessons

The Bible offers symbols of a different kind. Biblical images are not in themselves objects of devotion but objects of instruction. These object lessons for the soul symbolize the way God works in our lives. It is striking that we are given no clue in the Bible as to the physical appearance of Jesus. When you think about it, the Bible says little about the physical appearance of people in the Bible. How a person looked was simply not of great concern to the biblical writers. But that doesn't mean that God was insensitive to visual impact. The Gospel writers were very good at describing the life of Christ in ways that help us understand the *significance* of the events portrayed. They draw our attention to the action of Jesus rather than the appearance of Jesus. The baptism of Jesus by John in the river Jordan is pictured in a way that puts us on the scene. It is not a frozen still life or a portrait of a pristine personality. In our mind's eye we see a dynamic exchange between John and Jesus, and we visualize the baptism. We sense the humility of this act of surrender. The baptism has visual impact that immerses our senses. We are moved by the experience.

Throughout the Gospels the reader's attention is drawn away from static portraits to symbolic images. Jesus used the everyday objects around him, such as water, bread, sheep, vines and seeds, to get people's attention. He used powerful visual symbols to help us get a handle on how God works. God doesn't endow them with magical power, but God does use these common enough objects to stimulate powerful memories that shape our understanding of how he works. They are so mundane and earthy that they are easily overlooked. It is as if God chose these symbols so that we would never be tempted to turn them into idols. We can't do anything with these things to make them more special.

There is an aversion throughout the Word of God and the history of God's people to turning objects into idols. We would never make an idol of mere stones or bread or thorns. We would never fondle them or kiss them or cover them with gold or set them up as shrines. God knew that, and that is why he chose them. They are pointers directing us to the way the Lord works. Think of these symbols as shorthand notation for God's modus operandi. They are the Bible's iconoclastic images; they resist religious abstraction and beautification. Their significance and beauty reside in the memory of God's will that they instill within us.

The shepherd's staff is a good example. There is nothing quite so ordinary and simple as this basic wilderness tool. If we're not careful, we pass over this biblical image without seeing its significance. It fits into the environment so well that we take it for granted. Yet the Lord God transformed the staff in the hand of Moses into a powerful symbol of divine authority.

Excuses

The life of Moses is so large and full of significance that it is hard to imagine that we have anything in common with him. That is, until he opens his mouth. As soon as he starts to talk, he sounds just like us. To listen to his excuses is to hear ourselves talking back to God. He doesn't say anything that most of us haven't already said to God— many times. Like Moses our minds immediately run to all the reasons for not surrendering our lives to God. We counter everything God says to us with a quick excuse. When God called Moses, the wilderness shepherd responded with at least five excuses, all of which have been stubbornly used by believers throughout the centuries to dodge the discipline of surrender.

"Wrong number" excuse. As soon as God said, "Moses!" the prince-turned-shepherd was ready to tell God to call another number. You've got the wrong number! "Who am I, that I should go to Pharaoh and bring the Israelites out of Egypt?" (Ex 3:11). Recently our church administrator called a woman who answered the phone pleasantly but

unusually. Before he had a chance to say anything, she said, "Hello, you've got the wrong number. If you dial 555-6789 you'll reach the person you want." He responded, "Okay, then if I call that number, I'll reach Jane Smith?" "Oh," she said, "I'm Jane Smith. I get so many wrong numbers that I'm always prepared to give them what they need right away."

Moses was sure that God had gotten the wrong number. What could God want from him? He was so concerned about his own little "I" that we have to wonder if Moses had truly heard the "I" statements of God: "I am the God of your father, the God of Abraham, the God of Isaac and the God of Jacob. . . . I have indeed seen the misery of my people. . . . I have heard them crying out because of their slave drivers, and I am concerned about their suffering. . . . I am sending you to Pharaoh to bring my people the Israelites out of Egypt" (Ex 3:6-7, 10). Did Moses honestly believe that he could avoid becoming involved in God's will by feigning anonymity? I feel like saying, "Excuse me! Moses, this isn't about you. It's about God and his people. This isn't about a job and your résumé. You should be way past arguing job description!"

When God calls us, do we try to tell him that he has the wrong number? God says, "I've seen the confusion of your family, the brokenness of your home. I want you to be a Christ-centered servant-leader in your family." And you say, "Who, me?" And God says, "Yes, you!" God never expected or wanted Moses to think that he could do this on his own, and we can never do God's will on our own either. "I will be with you" is God's answer to Moses and to us (Ex 3:12).

"Let's talk about it" excuse. Moses illustrates a common trait among God's people when he says, "Suppose I go to the Israelites and say to them, 'The God of your fathers has sent me to you,' and they ask me, 'What is his name?' Then what shall I tell them?" (Ex 3:13). We prefer to talk about God's will rather than do God's will. "Let's suppose" is an infamous delay tactic. We subject the will of God to our hypothetical problems. We don't witness for Christ because someone might ask us a question we can't answer. We don't stand up for the commands of God

because we don't think we can defend them. We're not mature enough or deep enough to get out there and do God's will. We prefer to talk about it or, even better, listen to it being talked about. When it's all talk, somehow we don't feel responsible.

Again God wasn't buying Moses' excuse. If ignorance was his problem, God was perfectly capable of giving him wisdom. If Moses had questions, God had answers. "I AM WHO I AM. This is what you are to say to the Israelites: 'I AM has sent me to you' " (Ex 3:14). This is true for us as well. Our false humility that claims we're ill equipped for service is nothing but an excuse. God will give us what we need to obey his will. The apostle Paul was right: "For the kingdom of God is not a matter of talk but of power" (1 Cor 4:20).

"What if" excuse. And then Moses played the why-try-if-you-know-it's-going-to-fail card. When God won't be refused, blame others. Make your obedience contingent on the untried response of others. That's what Moses did, but God wouldn't be dissuaded. "What if they do not believe me or listen to me and say, 'The LORD did not appear to you'?" (Ex 4:1). Since when did our response to God's call depend on other people's response? Whether we will follow God's will for our lives cannot be based on what other Christians do, much less what popular culture does. Joshua said it well: "But as for me and my household, we will serve the LORD" (Josh 24:15).

"Woe is me" excuse. Only after challenging God's command, feigning ignorance and blaming others for how they might react did Moses claim incompetence. His next excuse implied that God's work required his ability to perform and that success was dependent on his skill. "O Lord, I have never been eloquent, neither in the past nor since you have spoken to your servant. I am slow of speech and tongue" (Ex 4:10). Does God's work rest on human abilities? Was God's will dependent on Moses' ability to persuade and communicate? No, and there would have been a problem if Moses had thought of himself as well qualified for the task. Remember what Paul said: "My message and my preaching were not with wise and persuasive words, but with a demonstration of the Spirit's power, so that your

faith might not rest on men's wisdom, but on God's power" (1 Cor 2:4-5).

"Can't you find someone else" excuse. The final excuse came out as a plea: "O Lord, please send someone else to do it" (Ex 4:13). We receive the distinct impression that Moses had finally arrived at his bottom line. If the truth be told, he just didn't want to be involved. In spite of God's call, God's backing and God's power, Moses was afraid. The will of God required that he face up to his feelings of inadequacy, but he wasn't prepared to do that.

Ginny, my wife, was assigning to her second graders parts for a school play when one of the boys pulled her aside and whispered, "Excuse me, Mrs. Webster, but I don't do anything that makes my heart beat faster." The comment was especially cute coming from a second grader because we have all known that adrenaline rush. It is easy to get in the habit of avoiding the pressure that comes from God's call.

It is amazing what people will do for themselves but refuse to do for God. Many go to great lengths to live an adventuresome life, but to risk their life for the sake of Christ would be unthinkable. Recently on TV I saw an attempt to break the world's record for having the most skydivers come together in a midair formation. On their third attempt some 240-plus skydivers broke the record. They held on to each other in formation for fifteen seconds. The feat, however, came at a terrible cost. On the second attempt a mother of two, who was in her thirties, inadvertently ran into another skydiver and was knocked unconscious. Unable to open her chute, she fell to her death. The skydivers solemnly dedicated their record-breaking jump to their fallen friend.

People are capable of the most amazing feats of self-discipline and risk-taking for relatively insignificant causes. They will devote themselves to their ego goal at the expense of time, money and family just so they can prove something to themselves. For the sake of adventure and the thrill of competition they're willing to sacrifice their lives. They eagerly give up everything for the sake of their pursuit.

My point is this: if people are capable of life-sacrificing passion for their ego goals, why can't we, as Christ's followers, surrender ourselves to God? If people will risk their lives to climb Mount Everest, why don't more Christians risk their reputation at work for the sake of the gospel? If the world can pursue its goals with such passion, you would think that Christians could honor God with as much conviction and passion.

A Staff

In the process of reasoning with Moses the Lord asked him a question. Given the situation it was a remarkable question. "What is that in your hand?" Of course God knew what Moses held in his hand, but the Lord asked the question anyway. "A staff," Moses replied. It was a common wilderness tool. Every shepherd had one. No one would usually draw attention to a staff. A staff was an all-purpose tool. It was a crutch, a weapon, an extension of one's reach and a means of rescue all rolled into one indispensable instrument.

> The LORD said, "Throw it on the ground."
> Moses threw it on the ground and it became a snake, and he ran from it. Then the LORD said to him, "Reach out your hand and take it by the tail." So Moses reached out and took hold of the snake and it turned back into a staff in his hand. (Ex 4:3-4)

The Lord suddenly transformed a common, ordinary staff into a snake. The God of molecular biology and atomic energy transformed the molecules of wood into a snake and then back again. The staff was not turned into a magic wand but into a snake.

> "This," said the LORD, "is so that they may believe that the LORD, the God of their fathers—the God of Abraham, the God of Isaac and the God of Jacob—has appeared to you." (Ex 4:5)

From then on this staff was to become a symbol of God's power. It was by this staff that God brought the plagues, one by one, to torment Israel's oppressors. Moses stretched out his staff and the rivers became blood, the dust became gnats, thunder roared and hail and lightning

struck the land, and locusts covered the ground. Moses was commanded to use his staff to part the Red Sea so the Israelites could
cross over on dry ground. When the Israelites grumbled and complained because they had no water, God said to Moses, "Take in your
hand the staff with which you struck the Nile. . . . I will stand there
before you by the rock at Horeb. Strike the rock, and water will come
out of it for the people to drink" (Ex 17:5-6). And when the Amale-
kites attacked Israel, Moses stood "on top of the hill with the staff of
God in [his] hands," and as long as his staff was lifted up the Israelites
overcame their enemies (Ex 17:9-11).

First of all we see that the staff represented God's power. It quickly
became a visible reminder of God's presence and power. In the hands
of Moses the shepherd's tool became an imprimatur of God's authority
that he designed to impress Israel. It also became a royal scepter used
to break the hard heart of Egypt's Pharaoh.

Yet the staff retained its humble status as a sojourner's tool. It represented a people on the move. When the Israelites ate their first Passover meal, they ate it in haste with traveling clothes on and staff in
hand (Ex 12:11). The emblem of God's authority never lost its down-
to-earth identification with the pilgrim's journey. The staff remained a
staff, even as it served as a symbol of God's presence and power.
When the Lord asked, "Moses, what is in your hand?" he underscored
an important principle. God can take the mundane, ordinary stuff
that makes up our lives and use it for his glory. The very things that
are close at hand are often what God intends to use (1 Thess 4:11).
We remain ordinary, but God accomplishes his extraordinary will
through us.

Finally, the staff was a constant reminder to Moses that he was
dependent on the Lord's strength and power. Moses was a person
under orders. Whatever power he manifested was a derived, delegated
power. He had no independent power to wield. "'Not by might nor by
power, but by my Spirit,' says the LORD Almighty" (Zech 4:6). Likewise the staff was a reminder to the people that God was in charge,
not Moses.

The shepherd's staff recalls the words of Jesus: "I am the good shepherd. The good shepherd lays down his life for the sheep" (Jn 10:11). Unlike Moses and King David, Israel's ultimate Shepherd was never literally a shepherd. But Jesus applied the metaphor to himself and fulfilled the meaning of the metaphor beyond any other image. This is why when we read the twenty-third Psalm, "The LORD is my shepherd, I shall not be in want," we think of Jesus. The promises of the psalm, "I will fear no evil, for you are with me; your rod and your staff, they comfort me" (Ps 23:4), are fulfilled in Jesus. There is only one occasion when we are told that Jesus specifically held a staff. This was after his arrest when he was paraded into the Praetorium to be mocked by Pilate's soldiers. Matthew describes the scene: "They stripped him and put a scarlet robe on him, and then twisted together a crown of thorns and set it on his head. They put a staff in his right hand and knelt in front of him and mocked him. 'Hail, king of the Jews!' they said. They spit on him, and took the staff and struck him on the head again and again" (Mt 27:28-30). The soldiers used a staff as a symbol of a royal scepter to mock and abuse Jesus. Little did they know then that the very one they were beating was none other than the Anointed One who will one day rule the nations with an iron scepter (Ps 2:9).

I believe the Lord still takes what is close at hand and uses it to manifest his glory and power. Instead of a staff, the Lord gives us the Holy Spirit, who empowers us to serve him faithfully. The Lord is not interested in hearing our excuses but in demonstrating his power through us. As we serve the living God, may our hearts beat faster!

4

Manna in the Wilderness

*He humbled you, causing you to hunger and then feeding you with manna,
which neither you nor your fathers had known,
to teach you that man does not live on bread alone
but on every word that comes from the mouth of the LORD.*

DEUTERONOMY 8:3

*M*anna *literally means "What is it?"* and was the name given by the
Israelites when they first saw this breadlike food. It was white like
coriander seed, tasted like wafers made with honey and mysteriously
appeared on the ground each morning. It was an appropriate name
because it meant so much more than food for the body. Manna was
also a symbol for the soul. They called it manna, but the Lord had
already called it bread from heaven.

Bread from Heaven

The *first* message to be found in manna was that there was more to
life than being well fed and physically satisfied. It didn't take long for
the Israelites to compare their existence in the wilderness to their

fond but distorted remembrance of life back in Egypt. "If only we had died by the LORD's hand in Egypt! There we sat around pots of meat and ate all the food we wanted, but you have brought us out into this desert to starve this entire assembly to death" (Ex 16:3).

Material gratification is a strong temptation that threatens long-term spiritual growth. If we allow it, foster it or give in to it, there can be a huge gap between daily life and eternal significance. It is hard for some people to grasp the relationship between living and meaning. One-dimensional existence misses the meaning of life. The great truths of God and salvation are ignored. Reducing life to appearances and appetites allows no vision for anything other than that which is literal, physical and material. Our dog, Maggie, lives this kind of one-dimensional life. She's fed twice a day, morning and evening. Science Diet dog food, a little exercise and affection make for a happy dog. We humans are in danger of living a dog's life when we say to ourselves, "You have plenty of good things laid up for many years. Take life easy; eat, drink and be merry" (Lk 12:19).

Satisfying our physical appetites at the expense of our soul is a major issue in the Bible. It is fine to care about our physical well-being, but we must care first and foremost about our relationship with the Lord. We need to eat and exercise, but there is more to living than following our physical and material appetites. This was the issue that confronted Jesus in the wilderness.

> After fasting forty days and nights, he was hungry. The tempter came to him and said, "If you are the Son of God, tell these stones to become bread."
> Jesus answered, "It is written: 'Man does not live on bread alone, but on every word that comes from the mouth of God.'" (Mt 4:2-4)

Jesus pointed back to the meaning of manna. He emphasized the priority of life in the Spirit over physical life alone.

To the Israelites, their Egyptian oppressors epitomized the good life. They had forgotten why God called Moses to deliver them: "I have indeed seen the misery of my people in Egypt. I have heard them crying out. . . . I am concerned about their suffering. So I have come down to rescue them" (Ex 3:7-8). They envied their oppressors and the very lifestyle that had made them poor. In the wilderness all they could remember was the all-you-could-eat Egyptian buffet. Looking back at their old way of life they seem to have forgotten the slavery and the misery. Often we are tempted to live only on the surface. When life is shrunk down to the tangible, visceral, physical and material world, it seems a whole lot easier to cope than to journey by faith in a real-world wilderness. The sad truth is that the Israelites began to talk as if they preferred humiliation under oppressive masters to humility before their merciful God.

Humiliation is the theme of Tom Wolfe's novel *A Man in Full*. Seven hundred pages on humiliation! We see character after character, from the super-rich real estate developer to the dirt-poor warehouse worker, experiencing humiliation in every way imaginable. According to Wolfe, life is humiliation, and there is no way around it. Whether we are high or low or in the middle, sooner or later we will be humiliated. Beyond that message Wolfe has nothing more to say. But the Bible does. The only way out of humiliation in the world is to have humility before God. The message is clear. James summed it up in a line: "Humble yourselves before the Lord, and he will lift you up" (Jas 4:10). The apostle Peter wrote, "Humble yourselves, therefore, under God's mighty hand, that he may lift you up in due time" (1 Pet 5:6).

The reason God allowed Israel to experience hunger in the wilderness was so Israel would learn to turn to God. But instead of praying to God for his provision they murmured and complained and wished they were back in their old lifestyle. God responded to their need in spite of their grumbling. They called it manna; God called it bread from heaven.

Food for the Soul

The Israelites questioned, "What is it?" but God's *second* message from manna was also clear. Manna was not only food for the body but food for the soul. From the start manna's purpose went beyond physical nourishment. God's physical provision was meant to be a reminder of their spiritual dependence. God put the Israelites on a healthy spiritual and physical diet. The Lord had no desire to compete with Egyptian cuisine. He fed them; he didn't spoil them. What a good diet can do for our bodies, manna did for the sojourners in the wilderness.

Over the last couple of generations there has been a revolution in the American diet. To prove the point, try getting teenagers to eat a big breakfast. In the movie *Pleasantville* two teenagers are transported back in time. They sit down to an old-fashioned Midwestern farmer's breakfast with piles of bacon, mounds of scrambled eggs and stacks of pancakes. Just seeing all that food was too much!

We have changed the way we eat. Tom Wolfe describes a sophisticated social party of Atlanta elites sitting down to an old-fashioned Southern plantation meal fixed by Aunt Bella, an experienced black cook. The main course was quail, served with Aunt Bella's own secret gravy, plus smoked ham, mashed potatoes, okra (gumbo), collard greens, snap beans boiled with ham fat and served with sliced onions and vinegar, and three kinds of pie for dessert. At the conclusion of this masterpiece the host invited Aunt Bella to come out and take a bow. She came out of the kitchen wiping her hands on a big workmanlike apron to receive her compliments. One of the women spoke up in a very ladylike Southern voice: "I don't know how you do it! To tell you the truth, I'm usually not crazy about okra, collard greens, and snaps, but yours just melted in my mouth. You've got to tell me your secret." Aunt Bella smiled broadly and let loose a laugh deep in her throat, and said: "Welcome to . . . Grease." Tremendous laughter broke out all around the table, except for the lady who asked Aunt Bella for her secret. She looked as though she had been shot through the heart.[1]

Americans have changed their eating habits, but Christians have also changed their spiritual habits. I don't mean to idealize the past, but I believe many Christians formerly took a much more serious approach to studying God's Word for themselves. They memorized the Word of God and prayed the psalms. They drew on the Word of

God daily. Many of us eat healthy and exercise often. We have become convinced that diet is a key factor in staying in shape and feeling healthy. But the concern that we have for proper physical nourishment has not carried over into concern for proper spiritual nourishment. We alternate between starving ourselves spiritually and eating a lot of spiritual junk food. A diet rich in Christian romances and end times fiction is like living on Big Macs and fries. They may taste good, but they're not that good for us. It is sad when so-called Christian publishers feed people's fantasies rather than their faith.

It truly would be well with our souls if we meditated on God's Word the way we attend to food. The biblical writers wanted us to link these two concerns together. As the psalmist said, "How sweet are your words to my taste, sweeter than honey to my mouth!" (Ps 119:103). The wilderness diet of manna and quail was designed by God to humble the people and focus their attention on him, their Creator and Lord. Just as an athlete's performance is related to diet and discipline, the depth of their worship was related to diet and devotion. The timing of God's provision emphasized daily dependence and sabbath rest. When considering food for the soul, these are two important issues. Daily dependence on God and participating in sabbath rest and worship are both designed to set the rhythm for the week.

Manna is an important reminder to me when I am inclined to worry about preaching. At times I'm burdened about the responsibility of preaching from week to week. I no sooner finish a message than I'm praying and thinking about preparing the next one. But two thoughts encourage me: first, the inexhaustible scope and depth of God's Word, and second, through the Holy Spirit, God will give me insight into his Word. I take the manna principle as a promise that God will provide in a timely fashion. If I depend on the Lord the way the Israelites depended on manna, I will never rise to preach the Word of God and have nothing to say. If we depend on the Lord, he gives us what we need in order to serve him. If we have too much, it leads to pride, and if we don't have enough, it leads to a false depen-

dence on others (or plagiarism when it comes to preaching). As the
proverb goes:

> Two things I ask of you, O LORD; . . .
> Keep falsehood and lies far from me;
>   give me neither poverty nor riches,
>   but give me only my daily bread.
> Otherwise, I may have too much and disown you
>   and say, "Who is the LORD?"
> Or I may become poor and steal,
>   and so dishonor the name of my God. (Prov 30:7-9)

The manna principle also underscores the need to seek God *daily*.
It may be important for us to ask ourselves some pointed questions: If
we have lost interest in worship or in fellowship with God's people, is
it because we lack daily fellowship with God? Are we confused over
God's will as it relates to work, finances and family because we don't
study his Word? Do we complain that Christians have let us down,
when in fact we have let ourselves down spiritually by refusing to
practice even very basic spiritual disciplines such as daily prayer and
Bible reading? In a preface to one of his devotional books Andrew
Murray wrote: "Meditate on this thought: The feeble state of my spiritual life is mainly due to the lack of time day by day in fellowship
with God. New life will dawn in many a soul as a result of time spent
in prayer alone with God."[2]

God gave manna in such a way as to reinforce the importance of
sabbath rest and worship. On the sixth day the people were to gather
twice as much so that they could rest on the sabbath. On other days,
if they gathered more than they could use, it spoiled, but on the sixth
day the surplus was preserved for provision on the sabbath. Even
though we live by the grace of Christ and not under the law, the sabbath principle is still important for Christians. This day of rest should
be set aside for renewal and reorientation. We need the reminder: "Be
still, and know that I am God" (Ps 46:10). We need to refocus on the
true meaning of our lives. Society has eliminated sabbath play and
rest by turning us into busy shoppers, fired up fans and overworked

employees. Religion has eliminated sabbath prayer and worship by turning Sundays into performances and committee meetings. It is our responsibility to obediently reclaim the day for health and holiness. When the Israelites first saw manna, they asked, "What is it?" They didn't realize at first that it was a sign of how God worked. For the Lord intended manna not only to be food for the body but food for the soul.

Bread of Life

The sustenance and symbolism of manna were well understood and memorialized by Moses and the Israelites. Manna was both bread from heaven—God's provision for their daily needs—and food for the soul—an object lesson of how God intended to work in their lives. Manna was part of God's spiritual conditioning program designed to humble the people and reveal their heart (Deut 8:2-3). Manna represented God's provision and purpose. "This is what the LORD has commanded: 'Take an omer [two quarts] of manna and keep it for the generations to come, so they can see the bread I gave you to eat in the desert when I brought you out of Egypt' " (Ex 16:32-33).

The *third* message from manna remained for Jesus to proclaim (Jn 6:30-51). Manna's greatest significance was that it pointed to Jesus as the Bread of Life. Following the feeding of the five thousand Jesus used Israel's wilderness experience to declare the truth about himself. The connection between ancient manna and the miraculous feeding of the multitude was not lost on the crowd. In fact, they brought it up.

> What miraculous sign then will you give that we may see it and believe you? What will you do? Our forefathers ate the manna in the desert; as it is written: "He gave them bread from heaven to eat." (Jn 6:30-31)

Jesus took this opportunity to fulfill the meaning of manna, which was intended by God from the beginning.

> "I tell you the truth, it is not Moses who has given you the bread from heaven, but it is my Father who gives you the true bread from heaven.

For the bread of God is he who comes down from heaven and gives life
to the world."

"Sir," they said, "from now on give us this bread."

Then Jesus declared, "I am the bread of life. He who comes to me
will never go hungry, and he who believes in me will never be thirsty.
. . . For I have come down from heaven not to do my will but to do the
will of him who sent me. . . . For my Father's will is that everyone who
looks to the Son and believes in him shall have eternal life, and I will
raise him up at the last day." (Jn 6:32-40)

In language reminiscent of the Israelites in the wilderness John continues:

At this the Jews began to grumble about him because he said, "I am the
bread that came down from heaven." They said, "Is this not Jesus, the
son of Joseph, whose father and mother we know? How can he now
say, 'I came down from heaven'?"

"Stop grumbling among yourselves," Jesus answered. "No one can
come to me unless the Father who sent me draws him, and I will raise
him up at the last day. . . . I am the bread of life. Your forefathers ate the
manna in the desert, yet they died. But here is the bread that comes
down from heaven, which a man may eat and not die. I am the living
bread that came down from heaven. If anyone eats of this bread, he will
live forever. This bread is my flesh, which I will give for the life of the
world." (Jn 6:43-51)

As a biblical object lesson, manna symbolizes God's complete provision. God meets our physical needs and our spiritual needs. From
the temporal to the eternal, God's provision is complete. It covers the
range of God's blessing from the Israelites' daily bread in the wilderness to the gift of salvation through our crucified and risen Lord.

Every time we break bread together, we remember that it is God
who strengthens our bodies and souls. There is an inseparable connection between the manna in the wilderness, our daily bread and the
bread of the Eucharist. When the Lord gave the Israelites manna and
insisted that they keep a portion of it in the ark of the covenant as a
testimony (Ex 16:33; Heb 9:4), he created a biblical image that
pointed forward to the Bread of Life. Jesus summed it up this way:

"Your forefathers ate manna and died, but he who feeds on this bread will live forever" (Jn 6:58). Therefore, whenever we "eat this bread and drink this cup, [we] proclaim the Lord's death until he comes" (1 Cor 11:26). We remember Christ's broken body, his sacrifice for our sin and his provision for our eternal salvation. God's provision is complete in Christ and meets all of our needs—body, mind and soul. "For the bread of God is he who comes down from heaven and gives life to the world" (Jn 6:33).

5

Gideon's Trumpet

The LORD said to Gideon,
"You have too many men for me to deliver Midian into their hands.
In order that Israel may not boast against me that her own
strength has saved her, announce now to the people,
'Anyone who trembles with fear may turn back and leave Mount Gilead.'"
So twenty-two thousand men left, while ten thousand remained.
But the LORD said to Gideon,
"There are still too many men. Take them down to the water,
and I will sift them for you. . . ."
The LORD said to Gideon, "With the three hundred men that lapped I will
save you and give the Midianites into your hands. . . ."
The three companies blew the trumpets and smashed the jars.
Grasping the torches in their left hands and holding in their right hands
the trumpets they were to blow, they shouted,
"A sword for the LORD and for Gideon!" . . .
When the three hundred trumpets sounded,
the LORD caused the [Midianites] throughout the camp to
turn on each other with their swords.

JUDGES 7:2-4, 7, 20-22

---

*G*od's strategy for success is different from ours. The world tells us to
believe in ourselves and expect great things, but God calls us to trust
in him and take up our cross. The world promotes pride, but God

instills humility. Motivational speakers inspire ambition, but spiritual directors encourage prayer. We feel our egos need all the help they can get, but God strips them clean. We add up our achievements, but God subtracts them one by one. Welcome to the discipline of surrender.

Reading the book of Judges is like entering a foreign world. Names and places are unfamiliar, and the customs and traditions seem crude and barbaric. High school history doesn't cover the Midianites and Baal worship. In the grand sweep of political history the Canaanite tribal conflicts in 1200 B.C. have little significance. Historians estimate that there were about 180 years between Joshua and King Saul (c. 1200 to 1020 B.C.). Scenes from the movie *Braveheart* come to mind. Or you might think of the era of Genghis Khan and the great Mongol invasions of Asia. Life was violent and cruel. It was a harsh and bloody world, a Darwinian world where the "survival of the fittest" was the order of the day. The only rationale preventing "ethnic cleansing" was the fact that dead people do not become slaves and raise crops. It was more profitable to dominate and oppress people and gain from their hard labor than to slaughter them. The powerful ruled the weak. Oppressors let the poor people plant crops, and then at harvest time they invaded the land to ravage it. This is what the Midianites did to Israel for seven years straight. Israel lived on the brink of annihilation.

The Gideon narrative begins by describing Israel's horrible oppression. Every year around harvest time the marauding Midianites descended on the Israelites, and the Israelites took refuge in mountain caves as their enemies ravaged the land. What was especially impressive were the Midianites' numbers. They were like "swarms of locusts," so many, in fact, that "it was impossible to count the men and their camels." It appears that the Israelites had to be pushed to this extreme crisis before they were willing to cry out to God. "Midian so impoverished the Israelites that they cried out to the LORD for help" (Judg 6:5-6).

The covenant of God's salvation seemed precarious, like a drowning victim about to go under for the last time. The patriarchs were few in number but strong in character. God established his covenant through Abraham, Isaac and Jacob. Joseph's relationship with God was exemplary and testified to the fact that God would keep his covenant and preserve the solidarity of Israel in a foreign and hostile culture. Four hundred years after Joseph died, the exodus from Egyptian bondage, led by Moses, proved to be a turning point in the history of God's chosen people. Joshua, Moses' successor, is remembered for his victories. He took Jericho, Caleb was victorious at Hebron, and Israel finally occupied the Promised Land.

But following Joshua's death Israel's history soured. Their spiritual resolve melted, and they looked more like their Canaanite neighbors than the covenant children of Abraham, Isaac and Jacob. The refrain "the Israelites did evil in the eyes of the LORD" introduces nearly every section of the book of Judges (2:11; 3:7, 12; 4:1; 6:1; 10:6; 13:1). It was a sad commentary on the people of God then; and down through the ages of salvation history many professing Christians have earned the same commentary.

God's Call

At this low point, when Israel was infiltrated from within by pagan practices and oppressed from without by powerful enemies, God intervened in two ways. He sent a prophet with a message and raised up a judge with a mission. The message might have been a stinging indictment—because Israel deserved it—but instead it was a call for understanding. God offered an explanation, not a tongue-lashing. We don't know how the message was received, but we know that Gideon responded as though he hadn't heard it.

The Lord appeared to Gideon and said, "The LORD is with you, mighty warrior." And Gideon replied, "But sir, if the LORD is with us, why has all this happened to us? Where are all his wonders that our fathers told us about when they said, 'Did not the LORD bring us up out of Egypt?' But now the LORD has abandoned us and put us into the hand of Midian" (Judg 6:12-13). Talk about attitude! He blamed

God for what had happened. Gideon refused to admit that the Israelites had brought it upon themselves.

Should we see any parallels here between our sorry state and our lack of obedience? Are we ready to challenge God's faithfulness when we have been unfaithful? We reap what we sow. As the apostle Paul wrote, "The one who sows to please his sinful nature, from that nature will reap destruction; the one who sows to please the Spirit, from the Spirit will reap eternal life" (Gal 6:8). We want to be taken seriously by the Lord, but sometimes it is good that the Lord doesn't take us so seriously! In spite of the provocative nature of Gideon's cynical criticism, the Lord simply ignored it and proceeded with his agenda. "Go in the strength you have and save Israel out of Midian's hand. Am I not sending you?" (Judg 6:14). Once again Gideon countered with a but. "But Lord, how can I save Israel? My clan is the weakest in Manasseh, and I am the least in my family" (Judg 6:15). Gideon's objection recalls Moses' protest, but the Lord continued, "I will be with you and you shall crush Midian as though it were a single man" (Judg 6:16 JB).

What follows is reminiscent of God's dealings with the patriarchs and with Moses. God gave Gideon a "burning bush" type experience (Judg 6:20-22). God made himself so real to Gideon that Gideon felt like he experienced nothing less than a face to face encounter with the living God. He was inspired to build an altar and worship. He called it "The LORD is Peace" (Judg 6:24). Then he went out, at God's command, and destroyed his father's altar to Baal and cut down the Asherah pole, a shrine to the fertility goddess. The town reacted by calling for his death, but Gideon's father intervened. "Let Baal fight his own battles" was his father's sentiment. "If Baal really is a god, he can defend himself when someone breaks down his altar" (Judg 6:31). There is a hint in his father's reaction that maybe Israel was ready to be done with nature gods and fertility cults. On that day they gave Gideon a new name, Jerub-Baal, which means "let Baal contend with him." Not a bad name for one who was about to lead Israel out of bondage. God took a relatively inconsequential, cynical and fearful

Israelite and gave him courage, assurance and responsibility. This is what the Lord will do for us if we allow him. This is what the Lord has done for many of us already. He has found us suspicious and cynical, and he has turned us around and given us purpose and meaning.

As the story builds and the showdown looms between the Israelites and the multitude of Midianites, the Spirit of the Lord came upon Gideon, and he blew a trumpet (a ram's horn), summoning his people to follow him and fight the Midianites (Judg 6:34). Yet even then Gideon continued to need reassurance that the Lord was on his side. He tested God's word with a wool fleece, not once but twice. The first time he wanted the fleece wet and the ground dry, and then he wanted the ground wet and the fleece dry. Each time God accommodated Gideon's request and proved himself. But just how much God was on his side was going to be proven in a way Gideon never anticipated. Gideon tested God, but God tested Gideon more. God wanted to remove not only Gideon's doubt but Israel's doubt. And even though he did it in a shocking way, we should not be surprised. It is the strategy of the cross.

God's Strategy

At the heart of the Gideon story is a radical battle plan. Israel was pitted against the camp of Midian. For seven years the hordes of Midian had descended on Israel, killing, plundering and ravaging the land. Now in the eighth year Israel finally had a leader in Gideon, who assembled an army of thirty-two thousand men at the spring of Harod. It was there that the Lord said to Gideon:

> You have too many men for me to deliver Midian into their hands. In order that Israel may not boast against me that her own strength has saved her, announce now to the people, "Anyone who trembles with fear may turn back and leave Mount Gilead." (Judg 7:2-3)

Twenty-two thousand men got up and left, leaving ten thousand to fight the Midianites. We can only imagine the consternation, let alone fear, at such a drastic reduction. We have no idea how Gideon explained troop reduction to those who remained. It defied all logic.

Who builds an army by subtraction? But God was not finished. The Lord said to Gideon:

> "There are still too many men. Take them down to the water, and I will sift them for you there. If I say, 'This one shall go with you,' he shall go; but if I say, 'This one shall not go with you,' he shall not go."
>
> So Gideon took the men down to the water. There the LORD told him, "Separate those who lap the water with their tongues like a dog from those who kneel down to drink." Three hundred men lapped with their hands to their mouths. All the rest got down on their knees to drink.
>
> The LORD said to Gideon, "With the three hundred men that lapped I will save you and give the Midianites into your hands. Let all the other men go, each to his own place." So Gideon sent the rest of the Israelites to their tents but kept the three hundred, who took over the provisions and trumpets of the others. (Judg 7:4-8)

If we try to discover some hidden military logic to this drastic reduction from thirty-two thousand to three hundred, we miss the point. We can discard all those theories that dwell on the difference between kneeling down to drink and bending over to drink. The object was not to pare down the ranks to a crack fighting outfit. This was not a special forces operation or an elite commando raid. No, not at all. The Lord wanted it obvious to Israel that they couldn't possibly win on their own.

Have you ever been tempted to reduce the ranks of the church down to those who really mean business with God—humble, mature, growing Christians? The thought can be tempting, but every effort to weed out the weak ends in failure. When it comes to building the church and proclaiming the kingdom, God does not seem to concentrate spiritual strength as much as disperse it. Judging from the Gideon precedent, God's purpose may be to manifest his strength in our weakness. The church in China is a prime example of this strategy. In the 1940s it looked like communism was going to wipe out the church. Many missionaries were sent home, some who stayed were killed, multitudes of Chinese believers suffered, and the church was severely persecuted. But far from dying, the church has grown significantly and has evidenced the powerful blessing of God.

God's strategy with Gideon recalls Noah, Abraham, Joseph and Moses, all of whom were outnumbered and would have been completely overpowered apart from God. It is consistent with how God worked with Elijah against the prophets of Baal, and with David against the Philistine Goliath. God's strategy has been the same down through the ages: "Not by might nor by power, but by my Spirit," says the Lord Almighty (Zech 4:6).

The same strategy is carried through to the cross.

> For the message of the cross is foolishness to those who are perishing, but to us who are being saved it is the power of God. . . . Brothers, think of what you were when you were called. Not many of you were wise by human standards; not many were influential; not many were of noble birth. But God chose the foolish things of the world to shame the wise; God chose the weak things of the world to shame the strong. He chose the lowly things of this world and the despised things—and the things that are not—to nullify the things that are, so that no one may boast before him. (1 Cor 1:18, 26-29)

All prospects of self-salvation are removed. Our deliverance comes from the Lord and the Lord alone. As the prophet proclaimed:

> "Let not the wise man boast of his wisdom
>   or the strong man boast of his strength
>   or the rich man boast of his riches,
> but let him who boasts boast about this:
>   that he understands and knows me,
> that I am the LORD, who exercises kindness,
>   justice and righteousness on earth,
>   for in these I delight," declares the LORD. (Jer 9:23-24)

The key phrase in the entire Gideon narrative is the line "in order that Israel may not boast against me that her own strength has saved her." This still holds true today. It is most definitely true when it comes to our salvation. We know we cannot save ourselves. It is also true when it comes to fulfilling the Great Commission and experiencing church growth. The question is whether we will cooperate with the Lord and put aside our human agendas of success and accept the divine principle of subtraction. The discipline of surrender runs against our natural inclination toward self-preservation and self-achievement. We are drawn to institutional pride, statistical goals, self-congratulatory rewards and motivational hype; but what is often missing is real worship, authentic Christ-centered spirituality and the principle of the cross. It is not enough to be well-intentioned, eager and enthusiastic for the work of the Lord. The issue is whether we can wait upon God and trust him. The look of self-oriented success concerns God because the feelings of pride are sure to follow.

Gideon's Victory

What happens when God takes away a sword and replaces it with a trumpet? You remember the story. Gideon assembled the three hundred who remained. He instructed them to follow his lead. At around 10 p.m. Gideon blew his trumpet, smashed his clay jar, held high a lighted torch and shouted, "A sword for the LORD and for Gideon." All three hundred Israelites surrounding the perimeter of the Midianite camp did the same thing. The reaction in the enemy camp was panic. Intelligence reports had indicated that the Israelites had no heart for battle. For several days they had been seen dispersing. Only a few hundred remained, and they were absolutely no threat to the huge army assembled in the valley. However, the enemy was not prepared for the element of surprise. Three hundred trumpet blasts, three hundred smashed jars, three hundred lit torches and three hundred shouts, "For the LORD and for Gideon," and all pandemonium broke out. Suddenly the valley, packed with troops and herds of camels, erupted. They turned on one another with their swords and fled.

The victory was the Lord's for sure, but Gideon's as well. The Lord called for action, took the initiative and gained the victory, but Gideon was right there as a faithful follower. The discipline of surrender did not lessen Gideon's involvement, it increased it. The Lord's action is at the heart of this history, but Gideon is in the story in a big way. He is no longer cynical but confident; no longer doubting but trusting; no longer fearful but faithful. To that end may Gideon's example inspire us. Too often the Lord finds us blowing our own horn! May Gideon's trumpet be a reminder that the battle is the Lord's, and he will win the victory. Whenever you hear an ordinary trumpet, remember that Gideon's God is your God.

6

The Easy Yoke

All things have been committed to me by my Father.
No one knows the Son except the Father,
and no one knows the Father except the Son and those to whom
the Son chooses to reveal him.
Come to me, all you who are weary and burdened,
and I will give you rest. Take my yoke upon you and learn from me,
for I am gentle and humble in heart, and you will find rest for your souls.
For my yoke is easy and my burden is light.

MATTHEW 11:27-30

The biblical images we have explored—the unadorned altar, the shepherd's staff, manna in the wilderness and Gideon's trumpet—symbolize an earthy, God-centered spirituality. These symbols retain their humility and point us to God. They communicate to the soul in a sign language that is easy to understand and remember. These objects of instruction memorialize true faith and dependence on the living God. The message they highlight is the spiritual discipline of surrender, which is submission to the will of God.

It is not surprising that our Lord Jesus Christ would also use object lessons to communicate the true character of spirituality. A particularly self-explanatory visual aid that he used was the farmer's yoke.

Even though we live in an urban culture, we know what a yoke is. True, we may have seen more pictures of oxen yoked together than actual sightings, but we know what a yoke is. It is a heavy bar, made of wood or iron, that holds two horses or oxen together so that they can pull a load or plow a field. It is not the kind of farming implement that draws attention to itself. It is all function and no fashion. It is about as glamorous as a trailer hitch! But it was an indispensable farming tool in Jesus' day that retains its symbolic value for us today.

Jesus used the yoke to call attention to the discipline of surrender: "Take my yoke upon you and learn from me" (Mt 11:29). Now let me ask you a personal question: Do you believe that you are yoked to Jesus Christ? The reason I ask this question is that if you don't honestly believe that you are yoked to Christ, you are missing out on the substance and depth of the Christian life. In the realm of discipleship, maturity and Christ-centered spirituality the yoke is something primarily seen and experienced rather than talked about. Our words will come across as very empty and shallow if our way of life is self-directed rather than Christ-dependent. For if there is any place we should be, it is under the yoke of Christ.

What Does It Mean to Take On the Yoke of Christ?
Living under the yoke of Christ is by invitation, not imposition. Christ does not impose a burden on us but invites us to follow him and live under his leadership. Christian maturity comes when we surrender our lives to God. Yes, it is by invitation only, and all of us are invited! Why would any Christian debate accepting the Lord's calling? Isn't this the most obvious choice? Yet many do debate this invitation and turn it into a dilemma rather than a blessing. They come to Christ, or think they do, but then they end up living independently of Christ. They say they believe, but they don't follow the teaching of Jesus. This real-world indifference to practical obedience to Christ is so hard for me to understand. By all counts we witness, as does the world, a huge gap between claiming faith in Christ and living lives committed to Christ in faithfulness and obedience.

All of us fight the tendency to cling to a lot of excess baggage that doesn't belong in the Christian life. The next time you're boarding a plane behind someone who is arguing with the flight attendant about carrying on his or her oversized, overweight luggage, think about the burdens you impose on your walk with Christ. Think about all the possessions, activities and habits that get in the way of following Christ and living under his easy yoke. Sometimes we insist on trying to travel the Christian life with all our personal baggage of guilt, materialism, lust and selfishness.

When we read the apostle Peter's admonition to cast our anxiety on Christ because he cares for us (1 Pet 5:7), we should remember that our Lord is our Savior, not our Sherpa. Sherpas are the rugged mountain guides from Nepal that guide adventurers up Mount Everest. For a fee they will risk their own lives to serve as expert mountain guides and beasts of burden. Jon Krakauer, in his personal account of a Mount Everest disaster, describes the load a Sherpa named Lopsang carried for the millionaire socialite Sandy Pittman. Lopsang hauled to base camp an eighty-pound burden, which included a satellite phone, two IBM laptops, a video camera, three 35mm cameras, a digital camera, two tape recorders, a CD-ROM player, a printer, an espresso maker, and enough solar panels and batteries to power the whole project.[1] Pittman trying to climb Everest with all her equipment is a picture of the Christian trying to follow Christ but still hanging on to all the cares and pressures of the world.

Jesus gave his life so that we might be free from the burden of sin and death. We cannot choose a materialistic lifestyle and rat-race existence and then expect to experience the blessings of Christ. We were meant to leave our burdens at the foot of the cross and follow Christ under his guidance. One of the practical ways you and I can measure how much of an unwarranted burden we are bringing into our relationship with the Lord is whether we can honestly say with the apostle Paul, "I have been crucified with Christ and I no longer live, but Christ lives in me The life I live in the body, I live by faith in the Son of God, who loved me and gave himself for me" (Gal 2:20).

Can we say this truthfully as we plan our schedules, parent our children, spend our money and work on our relationships? Jesus said, "If you hold to my teaching, you are really my disciples. Then you will know the truth, and the truth will set you free" (Jn 8:31-32). To be yoked to Christ is to be connected to the Master who will guide us in ways that are true and wise.

Living under the yoke of Christ is not difficult to figure out. It is unambiguous and straightforward. It is clear and not confusing. We must not make a mystery of what Jesus has communicated in a clear and compelling manner. It doesn't require a high IQ to figure out what God has in mind for a meaningful life. This is not like a complicated math problem that we just can't get. A little girl in my wife's second grade class was having a terrible time with math one week. The child loves reading, but she can't catch on to math. When she got her exercise back with many corrections, she immediately went to Ginny and said, "I just have to read. Please let me go and read. I'll sit in the corner and read." I empathize with that second grade girl because there are all sorts of academic and technical things that I don't get. But when it comes to the Word of God, the clarity and goodness of the truth are self-evident. Comprehending the truth of God is a matter not of intellect but of the will. It comes down to a choice.

The spiritual life is at the center of everything we experience, from worship to work and from relationships to recreation. Knowing God in the depth of our souls as well as in the midst of our daily schedules is a matter of simple obedience and trust. In other words, knowing God's will is not like doing our taxes. We don't have to spend hours and days working on figuring it out. The challenge to trust and follow him is a matter of obedience and surrender. It engages the mind and heart. Theology is important, and I would not want to minimize the importance of the mind, but the real issue is our willingness to yield to God's wisdom, to yearn for God's love, to submit to his will and to surrender to his call. To live under the yoke of the Master is to be in partnership with the Lord Jesus. We are called to learn from him and faithfully follow him. We pay attention to how Jesus does things. We believe that to know Christ is to become like Jesus. I like the way Max Lucado puts it: "What if everybody in our church made it their goal to be like Jesus?" In other words, "If I walked like Jesus, where would I go? If I knelt like Jesus, when would I kneel? [How would I pray?] If I had eyes like Jesus, what would I see? A mind—what would I think?" Lucado says, "God loves you just the way you are, but he doesn't want to leave you there. He wants you to be just like Jesus."[2]

The Sermon on the Mount is a powerful and concise summary of what it means to live under the easy yoke.

Beatitude-based character (Mt 5:1-12). Jesus' eightfold description of the person who is blessed is a reminder to us that we are meant to become nothing more or less than beatitude Christians. The beatitudes celebrate the life we have received, not the life we have achieved. They remind us of God's providence, not our performance. Under the yoke of Christ we find ourselves always moving forward according to this description. We never grow out of spiritual poverty, repentance, humility and hunger. We practice the spiritual disciplines of mercy, purity, peacemaking and perseverance. This is who we are in Christ, not what we were in sin.

Salt and light impact (Mt 5:13-16). Having pronounced the blessing, Jesus declares our responsibility. Having established our identity, he describes our influence by using salt and light metaphors to describe the difference Christ makes in our lives. To be a follower of Christ is to live a life that is impossible to conceal. It impacts everything, from family to work, from sexuality to spirituality. As salt prevents decay, light dispels darkness. Preservation and illumination describe the influence of the Christian in the world. We don't remove the yoke of Christ before stepping into the office or the classroom or socializing with our friends. To follow Jesus is to be under the yoke of Christ twenty-four hours a day. When we choose to live this way, representing Christ becomes easy in the sense that it is normal and natural rather than artificial and awkward.

Life-shaping dependence on the Word of God (Mt 5:17-20). Jesus came to lead us into faithful obedience to the commands of God's

Word. Jesus came not to abolish the law but to draw out the significance of the law and to fulfill all that God intended through the law.
Jesus came to establish the law, not undermine it; to complete it, not
condemn it. Religion substitutes external religious conformity for
true, heartfelt obedience. The easy yoke is all about learning to obey
God's Word from within. Obedience should not be reduced to a list of
do's and don'ts. It is deeper and more heartfelt and soulful than a legal
checklist. We desire to express our love for the Lord through humble
obedience.

Heart righteousness (Mt 5:21-48). Jesus' revolutionary strategy for
living, "You have heard it said . . . but I say to you," highlights a way
of life that is contrary to both religious and secular thinking. Jesus
revealed the visible righteousness characteristic of his yoked followers: the down-to-earth, practical faithfulness of love instead of anger;
purity instead of lust; fidelity instead of infidelity; reconciliation
instead of retaliation. The apostle Paul captured the essence of this
section of the Sermon on the Mount when he wrote:

> The acts of the sinful nature are obvious: sexual immorality, impurity
> and debauchery; idolatry and witchcraft; hatred, discord, jealousy, fits
> of rage, selfish ambition, dissensions, factions and envy; drunkenness,
> orgies, and the like. . . . But the fruit of the Spirit is love, joy, peace,
> patience, kindness, goodness, faithfulness, gentleness and self-control.
> Against such things there is no law. Those who belong to Christ Jesus
> have crucified the sinful nature with its passions and desires. Since we
> live by the Spirit, let us keep in step with the Spirit. (Gal 5:19-25)

Hidden righteousness (Mt 6:1-18). Jesus takes us below the surface
of religious appearances and explores the interior of our souls. He
wants us to distinguish between the artificial and the real in our relationship with our heavenly Father. Beatitude-based obedience and
salt-and-light impact are found in the hidden righteousness of personal communion with God. Who we are in public is vitally connected to personal spirituality. Giving to the needy, praying to God
and fasting are intended to strengthen our communion with God.
Spirituality that is practiced for the praise of others is false piety. True

spirituality is meant for God's "eyes" only! Then and only then do our acts of righteousness have enduring impact among others. The Puritans expressed this idea as living as if they stood before an audience of One. Ultimately the only opinion that mattered to them was God's. The principle of "the audience of One" meant that they lived to please God and God alone. As the apostle Paul said, "Whatever you do, whether in word or deed, do it all in the name of the Lord Jesus, giving thanks to God the Father through him" (Col 3:17).

Kingdom of God priorities (Mt 6:19—7:12). Jesus faced our issues of personal ambition, vision and devotion head-on. First, what are we living for? "Where your treasure is, there your heart will be also" (6:21). Second, what is the focus of our attention? "If your eyes are good, your whole body will be full of light" (6:22). And third, whom are you serving? "No one can serve two masters" (6:24). Jesus' easy yoke exposes the false dynamics that often accompany religious zeal: excessive worry, judgmentalism, manipulative evangelism and pious performance. Jesus calls for simple obedience, humble devotion and honest communion. Let's not make following Jesus more complicated than it needs to be. Jesus lightens the load and offers rest for the soul.

What it would take for us to live under the easy yoke (Mt 7:13-27). Jesus ended the Sermon on the Mount decisively, with layers of metaphor and admonition communicating a single message—a call for decision and action. Jesus closed with minisummaries, word pictures that visualized the truth and encompassed the message. Choose the narrow gate. Watch out for false prophets. Produce good fruit. Build your house on bedrock. Jesus warned us that the responsibility to choose wisely, discern carefully and act faithfully is ours and ours alone. Nothing is said or implied here to make it easier to choose the easy yoke. Jesus gives us either-or alternatives: two ways (broad and narrow), two teachers (false and true), two pleas (words and deeds) and finally two foundations (sand and rock). Either we are under the easy yoke or we are not. Either everything in life is integrated with our devotion to Christ or it is not. There are no shortcuts. Following Jesus becomes a heavy and confusing burden when it is lived only part-time or when it is approached half-heartedly. Choosing the narrow path does not sound easy, but it is a whole lot easier than the alternative.

We have all read and heard about the Jesus Seminar. It has been written about in major newspapers and magazines and discussed on radio and television. We've heard about the colored beads and what they signify: red for a quote from Jesus, pink for Jesus probably said this, gray for this sounds like something Jesus might have said, and black indicates what Jesus "definitely" did not say. My son, Jeremiah, raised an interesting point recently. He was in a college class that was discussing the Jesus Seminar. The question he raised was this: "Would there be much attention to the Jesus Seminar if Christians in America were suffering for their faith? Would this controversial academic speculation get any press if people were dying for their faith in Christ?"

Have we become used to "religion as usual" because we have not been encouraged or challenged to take up the yoke of Christ? Do we fall prey to the misery of our own burdens instead of the blessing and freedom of Jesus' easy yoke? Are we waiting for others to show us the difference that life under the easy yoke makes? I believe living under the yoke of Christ is an ongoing daily challenge. The easy yoke is a perfect metaphor for the discipline of surrender. We are invited to come under Christ's yoke and submit to his authority and power. It is not imposed on us as a burden but offered to us as a blessing. It is not a metaphor for hard labor but a symbol for empowered partnership. In this sense it is reminiscent of imagery found in the Psalms, such as "He who dwells in the shelter of the Most High will rest in the shadow of the Almighty" (Ps 91:1), and "He will cover you with his feathers, and under his wings you will find refuge" (91:4).

Jesus said, "If anyone would come after me, he must deny himself and take up his cross daily and follow me" (Lk 9:23). Too often we are burdened and weary with the cares and concerns of personal anxiety, ambition and agitation. We get down on others and ourselves, but we need to accept Jesus' offer to take up the easy yoke of Christ. We pay too much attention to the pressures of life when we should be paying attention to Jesus. "Take my yoke upon you and learn from me, for I am gentle and humble in heart, and you will find rest for your souls. For my yoke is easy and my burden is light" (Mt 11:29-30). The biblical image of the easy yoke reminds us that the discipline of surrender is not optional, it is a necessity. But blessing does follow, and God is faithful.

7

The Towel & Basin

Jesus knew that the Father had put all things under his power,
and that he had come from God and was returning to God;
so he got up from the meal, took off his outer clothing,
and wrapped a towel around his waist. After that,
he poured water into a basin and began to wash his disciples' feet,
drying them with the towel that was wrapped around him.
He came to Simon Peter, who said to him,
"Lord, are you going to wash my feet?"
Jesus replied, "You do not realize now what I am doing,
but later you will understand."
"No," said Peter, "you shall never wash my feet."
Jesus answered, "Unless I wash you, you have no part with me."
"Then, Lord," Simon Peter replied,
"not just my feet but my hands and my head as well!" . . .
"You call me 'Teacher' and 'Lord,' and rightly so, for that is what I am.
Now that I, your Lord and Teacher, have washed your feet,
you also should wash one another's feet.
I have set you an example that you should do as I have done for you."

JOHN 13:3-9, 13-15

It is amazing how a simple towel and a basin of water can symbolize
the very mind of God. These household items remind us not only of a
particular incident in the upper room but of God's way in the world.

They recall the humility of our Lord and Savior and the way of life we are called to practice in the world. All of the biblical images we have studied—the undecorated altar, the shepherd's staff, the wilderness manna, Gideon's trumpet and Jesus' easy yoke symbolize the way of the cross and the believer's dependence on God. On the night that Jesus was betrayed, he gave the disciples two object lessons: the bread and cup, and the towel and basin. Both symbolize the discipline of surrender.

Several months ago a friend gave me a framed and mounted black-and-white photograph of a towel and basin. A biblical text was printed under the picture: "All of you, clothe yourselves with humility toward one another, because, 'God opposes the proud but gives grace to the humble' (1 Pet 5:5)." This simple picture of a towel and basin is a powerful reminder of what it means to follow Jesus.

The walls of my son's room are covered with spectacular surfing pictures. My daughter has pictures of horses and golden retrievers everywhere. We like to visualize what is important to us. One of the most vivid scenes in the Gospel of John is when Jesus "got up from the meal, took off his outer clothing, and wrapped a towel around his waist . . . poured water into a basin and began to wash his disciples' feet, drying them with the towel that was wrapped around him" (Jn 13:4-5).

A Fresh Look

Not everyone understands the meaning behind this biblical image. Like other biblical images the towel and basin require *insider* information. Their meaning is not immediately accessible. Their significance lies in knowing how Jesus used each of these objects. If we separate them from who Jesus is and what he intended to teach us through them, they have little practical importance for us.

Like some of you, I have been a Christian for so long that I can forget what is new and startling to a person who is unfamiliar with the life of Christ. The image of Jesus on bended knee washing the disciples' feet may no longer impress us. Like some of the pictures in our homes, it is just there, and we no longer really see it. People who have become overly familiar with this picture of Christ may not be in a good position to explain its significance. What impresses others may no longer have an impact on us. We can be so used to Bible studies and sermons on Jesus washing the disciples' feet that this picture no longer stirs our souls. Therefore, both the seeker and the veteran believer need a fresh look at the details of this scene.

Before he described Jesus wrapping a towel around his waist and pouring water into a basin, John was eager to explain the significance of what was happening. He gave this picture of Christ a background and a caption. "It was just before the Passover Feast" places what is about to happen in the context of God's plan of salvation. And the caption under John's picture reads, "He now showed them the full extent of his love" (Jn 13:1). In framing the picture this way, John showed us that there is much more to this picture than meets the eye!

The Mind of Jesus

The apostle John was very concerned that we understand the full significance of what was happening. He guarded against a "dumbing-down" interpretation by stressing what was in Jesus' mind. "Jesus knew that the time had come for him to leave this world and go to the Father" (Jn 13:1); "Jesus knew that the Father had put all things under his power, and that he had come from God and was returning to God" (Jn 13:3). What Jesus was about to do must not be separated from his personal identity.

This incident is not about a great man condescending to do a menial task in order to inspire his followers to be humble. This is not a morality play for modern executives or a psychological experiment to gain employees' support. Secular interpretations of Jesus' actions must be put aside because this is all about what God has done for us. What is so simple on the surface, a mere towel and basin and the menial work of a slave, reveals the unfathomable mystery of God's great love and sacrifice. This is like the bread and wine in Holy Communion. It's not just about a meal together, it is about the Lord giving his life that we might live.

As Jesus took off his outer clothing and wrapped a towel around his waist, he knew he was "the image of the invisible God, the firstborn over all creation" (Col 1:15). As he washed the disciples' feet, he was conscious of his glorious destiny and his ignominious death, his universal sovereignty and his atoning sacrifice, his incarnate being and the burden of our iniquity. He who made human feet was willing to stoop to wash them! When Jesus deliberately dressed down, he dramatically portrayed his descent into humble service and sacrifice. The Creator humbly served the created.

This foot-washing scene has deep spiritual significance. It was primarily meant to picture the humility of God, not human humility. When John captioned this picture with the words "he now showed them the full extent of his love," he was pointing beyond foot washing to the cross. This object lesson of instruction was meant to prepare us for the meaning of the cross. On a human level, Eastern hospitality dictated the necessity of foot washing. On a divine level, God's justice dictated the spiritual necessity of soul cleansing by the blood of the cross. Are you prepared to allow God to show you the love that is in his heart? Are you willing to receive God's great gift of salvation? Are you willing to become a follower of Christ? The towel and basin symbolize much more than humble service—they symbolize the graciousness of God's offering and the extent of divine love. God himself is on bended knee.

Simon Chan, an Asian theologian, makes a sad but true observation: "Modern Christians proclaim *their* acceptance of Christ rather than Christ's acceptance of them!"[1] Meditating on the love of Christ restores our mind and heart to a right perspective.

Peter's Confusion

Peter didn't understand what was happening. He saw no connection between what Jesus was doing with a towel and basin and his Master's path to the cross. When Jesus came to him, Peter objected emphatically. "No," he declared, "you shall never wash my feet." Peter reacts much like those who expect Jesus to live up to their expectations. They don't conform to Christ; they expect Jesus to conform to their expectations. Their religion is what they find acceptable, what they deem important. When Jesus takes them out of their comfort zone, they object. Peter's refusal was surely well intentioned. He was not about to have someone he esteemed so highly wash his feet.

It wouldn't surprise me if there was someone like Peter reading this. You appreciate the exemplary character of Jesus and the wisdom of his teaching. You feel it is important to be religious and ethical. But you're not about to let Jesus deal with the dark side of your life. Jesus is on your pedestal of moral perfection, but you reject his sacrifice on the cross for your sin. In your mind Jesus is the American version of Buddha or Muhammad, a spiritual guide and hero, but he's not the Lord of the Universe, Creator and Redeemer. Peter looked up to Jesus, but he had no idea who he was looking at. He had no idea of the height and depth of the love of God. If this is true for you, I pray that you will hear with an open mind and heart what Jesus said to Peter, "Unless I wash you, you have no part with me" (Jn 13:8).

Of course, the meaning of Jesus' response had nothing to do with physical cleansing and everything to do with spiritual cleansing. The issue was holiness in Christ, not hospitality; the righteousness of Christ, not etiquette. Jesus was working out a parable that pointed to his sacrifice on the cross. At the time, Peter didn't understand what Jesus was getting at, but eventually he would (Jn 13:7). We think of this passage as an illustration about how we should respond to others. This is important, but before that lesson can be learned, we have to put ourselves in Peter's place. Are we willing to receive what Christ has to give us?

Peter's objection was undoubtedly well intentioned, but it was prompted by a false view of the Messiah and a self-righteous insistence on his own opinion. We feel embarrassed for Peter. He's stubborn, opinionated and defensive. He's always drawing attention to himself. But Jesus was patiently reasoning with him, saying, "Unless I wash you, you have no part with me." When Jesus put it that way,

Peter couldn't resist wanting a bath! We can picture an animated Peter immediately responding, "Then, Lord, not just my feet but my hands and my head as well!" (Jn 13:9).

Within a matter of hours Pilate had a basin and a towel brought out before the angry crowd. He washed his hands in front of the mob. The whipped-up rabble shouted, "Crucify him! Crucify him!" Pilate wanted his public hand washing to symbolize his innocence. He wanted to claim that he was not responsible for the injustice that he was about to approve. He was about to sentence an innocent man to death because of public opinion. The hand washing was a sham.

The contrasting pictures of Jesus washing his disciples' feet and Pilate washing his hands symbolize the two types of cleansing available to us. We can receive the cleansing that only God can provide, or we can insist on proclaiming our innocence in the face of our wrongdoing. We can receive from God or we can deceive ourselves. In the words of the gospel hymn, "What can wash away my sin? Nothing but the blood of Jesus."[2] And the apostle John declared, "If we confess our sins, he is faithful and just and will forgive us our sins and purify us from all unrighteousness" (1 Jn 1:9).

Do you know why God became incarnate and gave his life to give us life? When Peter looked down at Jesus, who was about to wash his feet, he was looking at none other than the Lord of the universe. It is this truth that is celebrated in Philippians 2:6-11:

> Who, being in very nature God,
>   did not consider equality with God something to be grasped,
> but made himself nothing,
>   taking the very nature of a servant,
>   being made in human likeness.
> And being found in appearance as a man,
>   he humbled himself
>   and became obedient to death—
>   even death on a cross!
> Therefore God exalted him to the highest place
>   and gave him the name that is above every name,
> that at the name of Jesus every knee should bow,

in heaven and on earth and under the earth,
and every tongue confess that Jesus Christ is Lord,
to the glory of God the Father.

Let This Mind Be in You

Before citing what many believe to be an early Christian hymn, Paul declared, "Your attitude should be the same as that of Christ Jesus" (Phil 2:5). The example of Jesus was meant to work its way into our daily lives and personal experience. This will never be done in a humanistic way—an ego-powered way—but it can be done in a Spirit-filled way. The towel and basin are symbols not only of Christ's sacrifice but of our own. The way to know Christ is to become like Jesus, through the power and wisdom of the Spirit of Christ. When Jesus finished washing the disciples' feet, he asked, "Do you understand what I have done for you?" (Jn 13:12).

When Eastern Orthodox believers use icons to worship God, they often make the sign of the cross and refer to the Trinity. They say aloud: "In the name of God the Father, Son and Holy Spirit." It is important for us to remember that apart from the power and wisdom and love of the Triune God, we will never grasp the meaning and practice of the Christian life.

We were meant to learn from the close relationship between Jesus' self-understanding and his self-sacrifice. When we know who we are in Christ, we experience the freedom and liberty to give ourselves in Christlike service. When we are unsure of our identity in Christ or when we misunderstand that relationship as Peter did, we experience so much trouble. If Jesus "knew that the Father had put all things under his power, and that he had come from God and was returning to God" (Jn 13:3), we should know that we "can do everything through him who gives [us] strength" (Phil 4:13). Jesus told us that in this world we will have trouble, but he said, "Take heart! I have overcome the world" (Jn 16:33). In other words, there is a parallel between Jesus' consciousness of the Father and our understanding of our personal relationship with God.

John introduced Jesus' action by saying, "He now showed them the full extent of his love" (Jn 13:1). This is important because it links foot washing and crucifixion. The everyday, mundane work of a servant is connected to the once-and-for-all sacrifice of the cross. For many of us, daily cross bearing looks more like foot washing than martyrdom. We are called on to sacrifice our egos more often than our lives. Life and death challenges are rare, but the way of the cross is ever before us.

It is out of the strength of your relationship with the Lord that you care for the practical, daily needs of others. You are washing the disciples' feet when you volunteer to work in the church nursery or when you visit a lonely, elderly person. You clothe yourself in humility when you dress down to feed the homeless or when you rush home from work so you can host a Bible study group. You are washing the disciples' feet when you labor all week to present the Word of God effectively to an adult Sunday school class or befriend a colleague who needs Christ.

As you think of ways that you wash the feet of others, think also of those who have washed your feet. Charles Plumb, a United States Navy fighter pilot, flew in Vietnam. On his seventy-fifth combat mission he was shot down by a surface-to-air missile. He ejected and parachuted into the jungle. Captured by the Vietcong, he spent six years as a prisoner of war before he was released. One day his wife and he were sitting in a restaurant when they were approached by a stranger. "You're Plumb!" the man announced. "You flew jet fighters in Vietnam from the aircraft carrier Kitty Hawk. You were shot down!"

Taken back, Plumb said, "That's right. How in the world did you know that?"

"Because I packed your parachute!"

Plumb gasped in surprise. The man shook his hand and added, "I guess it worked!"

"It sure did. If your chute hadn't worked, I wouldn't be here today."

That night Plumb couldn't sleep, thinking about the stranger. He

wondered how many times he might have seen him aboard the Kitty
Hawk but never talked with him because he was "just a sailor." The
careful work of the sailor, weaving the shrouds and folding the silks of
his chute, had saved his life.[3] Who is packing your parachute? Who is
washing your feet? It is important for us to ask, because our service is
the fruit of other people's sacrificial labor.

True biblical images retain their humility as they underscore the
principle of the cross. The towel and basin remind us of the discipline
of surrender. It is a simple picture that deserves to be remembered,
and a simple practice that needs to be followed for Christ and his
kingdom.

8

The Borrowed Donkey

As they approached Jerusalem and came to Bethphage on the
Mount of Olives, Jesus sent two disciples, saying to them,
"Go to the village ahead of you, and at once you will find a donkey
tied there, with her colt by her. Untie them and bring them to me.
If anyone says anything to you, tell him that the Lord needs them,
and he will send them right away."
This took place to fulfill what was spoken through the prophet:
"Say to the Daughter of Zion, 'See, your king comes to you,
gentle and riding on a donkey, on a colt, the foal of a donkey.' "
The disciples went and did as Jesus had instructed them.
They brought the donkey and the colt, placed their cloaks on them,
and Jesus sat on them. A very large crowd spread their cloaks on the road,
while others cut branches from the trees and spread them on the road.
The crowds that went ahead of him and those that followed shouted,
"Hosanna to the Son of David!
Blessed is he who comes in the name of the Lord!
Hosanna in the highest!"

MATTHEW 21:1-9

There is a right way and a wrong way to be passionate about Christ.
Not just any passion will do! In our eagerness to do something for
God, we all are tempted to ignore the way Jesus worked. We are sus-
ceptible to imposing our will, along with our fears and frustrations,

on the ministry of the gospel. I hesitate to say this because I don't want to sound negative, but I believe this biblical image is especially relevant to the church today. Wrong-headed religious activism is a great temptation and a hindrance to the ministry of the household of faith.

The apostle Peter is a classic example of what not to do! Remember how he took Jesus aside and rebuked the Lord for explaining how he must go to the cross. Remember too Peter's insistence on the Mount of Transfiguration that they construct three shelters for Moses, Elijah and Jesus. It was Peter who refused the Lord's foot washing and later struck the high priest's servant, cutting his ear off. Peter seemed especially prone to want to do something for Jesus whether it was in the will of God or not. Is the Lord impressed with our long-range plans and growth trajectories? Is a full calendar a sign of true spirituality? Many have carried the rhetoric of sports and business into kingdom work without asking if the Lord is really calling for a hurry-up offense or a full-court press. Somewhere along the line it became popular to apply market-driven, entrepreneurial zeal to evangelism and church growth. Ironically, we use words like *crusade* and *campaign* for evangelistic outreach even though such words conjure up images of aggression and conquest. Christian organizations are drawn to the corporate model. Secular advertising agencies are often used to promote the image of Christian ministries. Big donors are rewarded with luxury box seats at the Super Bowl and trips to the Holy Land with the organization's leaders.

I know of a wonderful evangelical church in Canada that is across the street from a major university. The church has a long history of Christ-centered preaching and global-mission concern. But first-time visitors are greeted with symbols of a bygone colonial era. The sanctuary is decorated with old flags of the Commonwealth nations. Students from developing nations, already sensitive to imperialism and colonialism, have to look beyond these symbols to see Christ. At best, the flag display is a distraction, and at worst it smacks of cultural pride and nationalism. The symbols that we proudly display may not be sending the message we want to be communicating. Our purpose is for people to see Jesus.

It is an understatement to say that we've strayed from our Lord's model. In our compulsion to do something big for God we seem oblivious to how Jesus worked. Proverbs warns, "It is not good to have zeal without knowledge, nor to be hasty and miss the way" (Prov 19:2). The apostle Paul wrote, "I can testify about them that they are zealous for God, but their zeal is not based on knowledge" (Rom 10:2). A fresh look at not only Jesus' actions but his methods is bound to challenge some of our preconceived notions of how to communicate the gospel. From the beginning to the end of his ministry, Jesus approached the world with a combination of humility and authority that was foreign to anything in the world. Jesus never took his cues from the world, much less from a marketing strategy. On the contrary, he demonstrated how the discipline of surrender applies to the communication of the gospel. He proclaimed the good news with confidence and humility, and surrounded his message with symbols that pointed to the cross. He offered a no-fear gospel with conviction and compassion, and deliberately distanced himself from any sign of worldly prestige and power. Jesus' verdict on triumphalism, that ego-gratifying, self-exalting, world-impressing approach to ministry, can be clearly seen in his triumphal entry into Jerusalem. Jesus intentionally chose to make his entrance on a young donkey, a sign of humility and gentleness. His journey to the cross was in direct fulfillment of Zechariah's prophecy:

> Rejoice greatly, O Daughter of Zion!
>   Shout, Daughter of Jerusalem!
> See, your king comes to you,
>   righteous and having salvation,
>   gentle and riding on a donkey,
>   on a colt, the foal of a donkey. (Zech 9:9)

How does this rate as a grand entrance? As a rule, auspicious events, from the president's state of the union address to the Olympics, do not begin with an evident sign of humility. Look at the Oscars if you want to see how celebrities make an entrance. Society rolls out the red carpet for the rich and famous. But for Jesus they took off their coats and spread them on the road. They gave him a spontaneous royal welcome but not in the tradition of Rome. By choosing a donkey Jesus stirred the people's imagination. They remembered the prophets and the word of the Lord through Zechariah. Rome symbolized the triumph of military conquest and aggression, but Jesus symbolized the grace of God. When Pilate's chariot raced through the city, the people got out of the way so they wouldn't be trampled. But when Jesus rode into Jerusalem on a donkey, they spread their coats and palm branches along the way. Unlike the Roman processionals, which were met with defiant stares and grudging acceptance, Jesus' triumphal entry was greeted with loud Hosannas. The Psalms were sung in the streets of Jerusalem: "Blessed is he who comes in the name of the LORD" (Ps 118:26).

Fulfilled Prophecy

Many Christians make the mistake of assuming that Jesus, because of his deity, knew everything about his messiahship. They do not take seriously what it meant for Jesus to make "himself nothing, taking the very nature of a servant, being made in human likeness" (Phil 2:7). Christians seem to find it easier to accept the fact that Jesus emptied himself of omnipotence but much more difficult to believe that he emptied himself of omniscience. They believe he was dependent on the Father for miraculous power, but they assume he knew everything there was to know because he was God. However, if we take the Bible seriously, we learn that the incarnate One intentionally limited himself physically and intellectually in order that he might fully assume our humanity. He was one with us in every way. As the writer of Hebrews says, "We do not have a high priest who is unable to sympathize with our weaknesses, but we have one who has been tempted in every way, just as we are—yet was without sin" (Heb 4:15). Jesus underscored this limitation when he discussed his return: "No one knows about that day or hour, not even the angels in heaven, nor the Son, but only the Father" (Mk 13:32).

When we grasp the biblical testimony about Jesus, we gain a deeper insight into his dependence on communion with the Father and his personal study of the Bible. Luke observed, "Jesus grew in wisdom and stature, and in favor with God and men" (Lk 2:52). The fully human Jesus submitted himself to a learning process not unlike our experience of growth and insight. Through prayer and Bible study he understood the true meaning of his messiahship. "Although he was a son, he learned obedience from what he suffered" (Heb 5:8). The witness of John the Baptist and the affirmation of the Father at his baptism, as well as the ongoing testimony of the Spirit of God, confirmed within Jesus his identity and mission.

One of the many prophecies that shaped Jesus' self-understanding was Zechariah's description of the coming king. Guided by the Spirit of God, Jesus wove together strains of prophecy about the Suffering Servant (Is 53) and the Conquering Messiah (Ps 2) into the beautiful tapestry of salvation history. At Christmas the symbol of the manger recalls Isaiah's prophecy:

> For to us a child is born,
>   to us a son is given,
>   and the government will be on his shoulders.
> And he will be called
>   Wonderful Counselor, Mighty God,
>   Everlasting Father, Prince of Peace. (Is 9:6)

The Palm Sunday picture of Jesus riding into Jerusalem on a donkey fulfills Zechariah's prophecy.

Jesus walked all the way from Galilee, but he chose to ride the last two miles in order to make a statement. The Prince of Peace approached Jerusalem in humility, riding on a donkey. He didn't come charging into town on a stallion but humbly rode on a colt that had never been ridden before. With its mother by its side, the young male donkey remained calm as the processional slowly moved through the noisy crowd. The festive atmosphere was charged with emotion and expectation. Men and women, boys and girls were singing in the streets. They were shouting "Hosanna in the highest!"

A Blue-Collar Beast of Burden

Jesus deliberately staged this demonstration. His directions were explicit: "Go to the village ahead of you, and at once you will find a donkey tied there, with her colt by her. Untie them and bring them to me. If anyone says anything to you, tell him that the Lord needs them, and he will send them right away" (Mt 21:2-3). His authority was as regal as his purpose was humble. He spoke as a sovereign, but he instructed his disciples to assure the owner of the colt and donkey that they would be sent right back. Whether prior arrangements had been made or this was a case of answered prayer, we do not know. Whether the owner understood that the request came from the Lord or a respectable individual, we do not know. What we do know is that the disciples found a donkey and her colt as Jesus had said and brought both animals to him.

Biblical images retain their earthiness long after they have been used to communicate powerful truths. They resist ornamentation and beautification. No one bows before a towel and basin or kisses a thorn. These objects of instruction were never meant to be turned into objects of devotion. This is certainly true of the donkey also. There is little temptation to see a donkey as anything other than an ordinary beast of burden.

The donkey captures, in a symbolic way, the humility of God's approach to us. The way Jesus rode into Jerusalem is the way God comes into our lives. His coming is invitational and celebrative, rather than intimidating and condemning. "Come to me, all you who are weary and burdened, and I will give you rest. Take my yoke upon you and learn from me, for I am gentle and humble in heart, and you will find rest for your souls. For my yoke is easy and my burden is light" (Mt 11:28-30). On another occasion Jesus likened himself to a hen gathering her chicks under her wings (Mt 23:37). From the beginning of his ministry Jesus embodied the invitation of

God. " 'Come now, let us reason together,' says the LORD. 'Though your sins are like scarlet, they shall be as white as snow; though they are red as crimson, they shall be like wool' " (Is 1:18).

The never-before-ridden colt, the festive crowd of families, the children shouting "Hosanna" and the elderly praising God create a wonderful picture of peace and joy. This is not the happiness of a theme park. No one is being entertained, and no one is trying to be religious. Real worship is taking place on the streets of Jerusalem. God continues to approach us in humility and gentleness with his gift of salvation. The real tragedy is that anyone would turn down his invitation.

Selling Jesus

Should we be as deliberate as Jesus was in choosing symbols that convey the gospel and as selective as he was in ruling out certain symbols that misrepresent the gospel? If we take the example of Jesus seriously, we will approach others with the gospel in humility and gentleness. We will shun symbols that seek to present the gospel by impressing others with wealth, clout and sex appeal. The donkey is a good reminder that a God-centered holy life is truly a human life, an ordinary, down-to-earth life. The lordship of Christ was demonstrated on the streets of Jerusalem and among the people. The biblical image of the donkey is a reminder to parents to relate to their sons and daughters with humility and authority. In the name of Christ our approach to people is characterized by compassion and conviction. As a pastor I must keep ever before me the image of Christ on the donkey heading toward the cross.

Let the borrowed donkey remind us of Jesus' lack of dependence on money to accomplish his work. When he was born, he was laid in a borrowed manger, and when he died, he was laid in a borrowed tomb. He owned nothing but was the Lord of all. As he said, "Foxes have holes and birds of the air have nests, but the Son of Man has no place to lay his head" (Mt 8:20). The message ought to be clear. Money is not the prerequisite to ministry that we seem to think it is!

George Müller, the nineteenth-century missionary, gained a reputation for depending on the promises of God. He challenged himself to trust the Lord for his material needs. When the Lord moved him to establish an orphan home, he wanted this ministry to demonstrate the faithfulness of God. Although it was his earnest desire "to help the poor children and train them in the ways of God," his "primary object" was to illustrate that God is faithful and answers prayer.[1] He and his wife prayed for a house, an operating budget and individuals who would take care of the children. In six months the Lord answered all of their prayers. But then the Lord taught him a valuable lesson.

Müller had been praying fervently for the material and financial needs of the orphanage, but he never prayed that the Lord would send them orphans. "I took it for granted," he admitted, "that there would be plenty of applications." But no applications came. He wrote in his journal, "This circumstance led me to bow low before my God in prayer and to examine the motives of my heart once more. I could still say that His glory was my chief aim—that others might see it is not a vain thing to trust in the living God."[2] The next day the orphanage received its very first application, which was followed in a short time by many more. One year later George and Mary Müller had sixty-four children under their care in two orphan homes. The Müllers learned the spiritual priority of waiting on the Lord for not only the material needs but for the children themselves.

The triumphal entry and the temple cleansing happened back-to-back, sending the same message against marketing the gospel. The very next day (Mk 11:12) Jesus went to the temple and "drove out all who were buying and selling there. He overturned the tables of the money changers and the benches of those selling doves" (Mt 21:12). He foreshadowed the day when the prophecy of Zechariah would be fulfilled. The Lord of the temple had driven out the merchants from the house of the Lord Almighty (Zech 14:21).

The young donkey serves as a symbol of peace, not war, reminding us that the battle is the Lord's (1 Sam 17:47). We were never meant to rely on "the chariots from Ephraim" or "the war-horses from Jerusalem" (Zech 9:10). As the apostle said, "The weapons we fight with are not the weapons of the world. On the contrary, they have divine power to demolish strongholds" (2 Cor 10:4). Today's disciples of Jesus still follow the Prince of Peace. The journey to the cross remains a procession marked by gentleness and humility. The picture of Christ on the donkey is a reminder to the church of how this journey should proceed. At the very center of Jesus' action was a remarkable calm. The power of God was made manifest in a picture of humility and surrender. Jesus was fully aware of what was going on. This is the model we want to follow as we grow up in Christ and seek to accomplish his will.

Faithful and True

The picture of the white horse in Revelation is in sharp contrast to the picture of Jesus riding into Jerusalem on a donkey. The only similarity between these two scenes is the rider. The triumphal entry will be consummated one day in judgment and justice. The approach of God on that day will be as fearsome and devastating as it was gentle and humble. Those who have spurned his love and rejected his salvation will be struck down. *Today* is the day to accept God's gracious invitation of salvation. The Lord, who is "Faithful and True," comes to us today with grace and mercy, a processional that symbolizes the peace and joy God seeks to give to us. The question is this: Will we condemn him from the sidelines or enter into worship with loud hosannas? "Blessed is he who comes in the name of the Lord!" (Mt 21:9).

> I saw heaven standing open and there before me was a white horse, whose rider is called Faithful and True. With justice he judges and makes war. His eyes are like blazing fire, and on his head are many crowns. He has a name written on him that no one knows but he himself. He is dressed in a robe dipped in blood, and his name is the Word of God. The armies of heaven were following him, riding on white horses and dressed in fine linen, white and clean. Out of his mouth comes a sharp sword with which to strike down the nations. "He will rule them with an iron scepter." He treads the winepress of the fury of the wrath of God Almighty. On his robe and on his thigh he has this name written:
>
> KING OF KINGS AND LORD OF LORDS. (Rev 19:11-16)

9

The Crowing Rooster

Then Jesus told them, "This very night
you will all fall away on account of me." . . .
Peter replied, "Even if all fall away on account of you, I never will."
"I tell you the truth," Jesus answered, "this very night,
before the rooster crows, you will disown me three times."
But Peter declared, "Even if I have to die with you,
I will never disown you." . . .
Now Peter was sitting out in the courtyard, and a servant girl came to him.
"You also were with Jesus of Galilee," she said.
But he denied it before them all.
"I don't know what you're talking about," he said.
Then he went out to the gateway, where another girl saw him and said to
the people there, "This fellow was with Jesus of Nazareth."
He denied it again, with an oath: "I don't know the man!"
After a little while, those standing there went up to Peter and said, "Surely
you are one of them, for your accent gives you away."
Then he began to call down curses on himself and he swore to them,
"I don't know the man!"
Immediately a rooster crowed. . . . And he went outside and wept bitterly.

MATTHEW 26:31-35, 69-75

*T*he early church made the crowing rooster a symbol of watchfulness
and vigilance. It reminded Christians of Peter's denial and repentance.
In this way the crowing rooster became one of the symbols of the cru-

cifixion. Early paintings of the apostle Peter show him holding the keys of heaven with a rooster pictured nearby to remind us of his denial. But the rooster does more than recall Peter's denial; it causes us to think of our susceptibility to pride, our fear of standing up for Christ and our vulnerability to denying Christ.

The Upper Room

Jesus' last extended conversation with the disciples lacked nothing. It had the character of full disclosure and intimate friendship. Jesus left nothing unsaid that should be said. He washed their feet and led them in the Last Supper. He spoke words of comfort—"Do not let your hearts be troubled. Trust in God; trust also in me" (Jn 14:1); "Peace I leave with you; my peace I give you. I do not give to you as the world gives" (Jn 14:27)—and words of challenge, "A time is coming when anyone who kills you will think he is offering a service to God" (Jn 16:2). Jesus promised them the Holy Spirit, and he prayed for them. He prayed that great glory prayer recorded in John 17: "My prayer is not that you take them out of the world but that you protect them from the evil one. They are not of the world, even as I am not of it. Sanctify them by the truth; your word is truth" (Jn 17:15-17).

Everything Jesus said that night was meant to prepare the disciples for what was coming. The future involved a deeper fellowship with God through an abiding fellowship with the Son: "I am the vine; you are the branches" (Jn 15:5). He promised the empowering comfort and counsel of the Holy Spirit and a growing realization of the glory of God the Father. Jesus prayed, "Father, I want those you have given me to be with me where I am, and to see my glory, the glory you have given me because you loved me before the creation of the world" (Jn 17:24). The future also involved betrayal, denial, persecution and death.

The emotional range of the upper room conversation was extreme, from "I tell you the truth, one of you is going to betray me" (Jn 13:21) to "I have called you friends, for everything that I learned from my Father I have made known to you" (Jn 15:15). Jesus was confident, encouraging and bold. "I have told you these things, so that in me you may have peace. In this world you will have trouble. But take heart! I have overcome the world" (Jn 16:33). But his tone was also ominous and sad. Jesus warned the disciples that they would "all fall away on account" of him. He quoted from the prophet Zechariah: "I will strike the shepherd, and the sheep of the flock will be scattered" (Mt 26:31, quoting Zech 13:7). The sober realization that he was about to be betrayed by Judas, denied by Peter and abandoned by the rest of the disciples did not distract Jesus from preparing and praying for all of his disciples, including us.

Betrayal and Denial

Judas and Peter invite comparison, but their situations are radically different. Jesus exposed Judas, but he warned Peter. He spoke of being betrayed to let Judas know that he was fully aware of his betrayer's deception and treachery. Judas's feigned innocence ("Surely not I, Rabbi?") thinly concealed a heart that had grown hard and resistant to Jesus. Judas hated Jesus, and Jesus knew it. He pronounced Judas's verdict even before he had committed the act: "Woe to that man who betrays the Son of Man! It would be better for him if he had not been born" (Mt 26:23-25). After the betrayal, we are told by Matthew, Judas was "seized with remorse." He tried to return the thirty pieces of silver. "I have sinned," he announced, "for I have betrayed innocent blood." "What is that to us?" the chief priests and elders replied. "That's your responsibility" (Mt 27:4). There is no indication that Judas had any attachment to Jesus other than a realization in the end that he had wronged an innocent man. According to the apostle Peter, Judas's remorse stopped short of repentance. His despair does not appear to have led to deliverance. The finality of suicide sealed Judas's tragic and willful determination. In the book of Acts it is Peter who brings closure to the Judas saga. He quotes from the Psalms to describe Judas's fate: "May his place be deserted; let there be no one to dwell in it" (Acts 1:20; see Ps 69:25). The disciples found it fitting that Judas should be memorialized by a cemetery known as the Field of Blood.

The difference between Judas and Peter is the difference between exposing a deceptive heart and warning a weak heart. It is the difference between contempt for what Jesus stands for and false confidence in one's ability to stand for Jesus. Treachery is different from timidity. Both may lead to sin, but being hateful is different from being hurtful. Judas wanted to expose Jesus as a fraud, but Peter wanted to be faithful to Jesus. Judas was filled with regret, but Peter was filled with repentance. We are meant to see ourselves in Peter, but no one was ever meant to identify with Judas.

Close to the Edge

A crowing rooster should remind us not only of Peter's denials but of how much we are like Peter. As one writer said, "All disciples can profit by a careful study of how the 'Rock' turned to 'sand' in his most critical test."[1] When I study Peter, it makes me nervous. It's like standing real close to the edge of Niagara Falls. Peter played it too close to the edge, and he fell. If Peter, the representative disciple and a member of Jesus' inner circle, could fall, so can I. The nature of Peter's experience is too close to our own to be ignored. His vulnerability to sin reminds us of our own. We find it easy, all too easy, to identity with him. Many of us share his pride, practice his brand of foolishness and experience his lack of courage and faithfulness.

Peter's pride was so transparent that we find ourselves both embarrassed for him and angry at him. He is an outstanding illustration of the proverb: "Pride goes before destruction, a haughty spirit before a fall" (Prov 16:18). When Jesus said, "This very night you will all fall away on account of me," Peter replied, "Even if all fall away on account of you, I never will" (Mt 26:31, 33). This bold, brash claim made by the impetuous, outspoken Peter gets our attention. There is nothing humble about the rhetoric of self-confidence. Peter's proud claim is like the pregame hype surrounding the Super Bowl. The media ritual that we have come to expect before a big game, with the chest-thumping display of one-upmanship, is a parody of Peter's proud boast.

We instinctively ask, "How could Peter say such a thing?" With the rest of the disciples standing right there, Peter's single comment turned loyalty to Jesus into a competition with himself as the self-proclaimed winner (see Gal 6:4). Pride is insidious because it often separates us from reality and from others without our even knowing it.

What do you think would have happened if John had pulled Peter aside and said, "Will you get a grip? Listen to yourself! Where do you get off claiming to be better than the rest of us?" We don't read that John or any of the other disciples said anything to Peter. They let Jesus deal with Peter. The reason we are seldom confronted about our pride is because pride, although so obvious, is a tough sin to expose to the proud. Pride is a form of self-deception, and when we deceive ourselves, it is almost impossible for us to see the truth. Like Peter, we believe our own propaganda. Pride is often couched in spiritual terms. We claim that we know the mind of God on a certain matter and that others don't. We equate our feelings with God's heart. We preface what we have to say with "God told me" or "God laid it on my heart," and we think that if others only shared our perspective, then God would surely bless them. In effect, we falsely condemn others for not being as spiritual as we are. Peter would have been shocked to be confronted over his sin of pride. What he felt was courage, loyalty and boldness for Jesus, we realize was pride! Our pride often runs its course and leaves us disillusioned and frustrated. What sounded so spiritual turns into denials and curses. We feel abandoned by God, when in fact, it is we who have abandoned God by putting ourselves first. Instead of waiting and watching and depending on the Lord, we have trusted in ourselves.

Peter's courage depended on an ego challenge rather than a spiritual challenge. I believe under certain conditions Peter would have made good on his claim to lay down his life for Jesus (Jn 13:37). The evidence for this can be seen in the garden of Gethsemane. When Peter was confronted, he reacted by fighting back. As you might expect, if only two disciples were armed, one of them would have to have been Peter (Lk 22:38). Peter drew his sword and cut off the ear of the high priest's servant. Immediately Jesus commanded Peter, "Put your sword away! Shall I not drink the cup the Father has given me?" (Jn 18:11). Why was Peter willing to risk his life in hand-to-hand combat in the garden but fearful to admit to a servant girl that he knew Jesus? This doesn't appear to make sense until we realize the nature of the conflicting challenges.

In the garden it was a challenge to Peter's bravery, his willingness to fight and his readiness to put his life on the line for the cause. Peter was up to the ego challenge. But alone in the high priest's courtyard, with no surrounding audience, Peter was unwilling to admit that he was one of Jesus' disciples. When his own ego was not in question and his macho image was not threatened, Peter found it easier to deny that he even knew Jesus. The servant girl got from Peter what an armed centurion would have been unable to extract—a denial! She made it easy for him: "You are not one of his disciples, are you?" (Jn 18:17).

In a sanctuary surrounded by brothers and sisters in Christ, we are brave souls, but put us in a university classroom or a teacher's lounge or in an office or a social gathering and it's easy to see how denial happens. "Surely you don't believe in this Jesus stuff, do you?" The world begs for our agreement, and it's easier to agree than to make a stand. In word or deed we deny him and break the heart of our Savior and Lord.

What if Peter had not boasted after Jesus had warned the disciples that they were all going to fall away? What if he had said, "Lord, we don't want to fall away! How can we prevent it?" We have a good indication of how Jesus would have answered that question from his response to the exhausted disciples in the garden of Gethsemane. He simply said, "Watch and pray so that you will not fall into temptation. The spirit is willing, but the body is weak" (Mt 26:41). If the disciples had returned to the upper room and spent the night in prayer, they would have felt more united than isolated. Instead of falling away they might have waited on God. Sadly, it wasn't until after the cross that they returned to the upper room.

Peter's denial was emphatic. He reinforced it with expletives and oaths. A hasty denial might have been said without thinking, and a second chance could have led Peter to reconsider. But instead his timidity grew, his resolve weakened, and he denied the Lord a second time with more conviction than the first. "I don't know the man!" he announced. By now Peter's rejection had worn a groove in his conscience. Having crossed the line twice, he didn't hesitate to lie and deceive with as much boldness as he was capable of. He called down curses on himself and announced his denial for all to hear. Once, it might have been a moment of weakness, quickly taken back. Twice, an unmistakable denial. Three times, an undeniable pattern of rejection.

A Wake-Up Call

The sound of the rooster crowing immediately brought to Peter's mind the words that Jesus had spoken: "Before the rooster crows, you will disown me three times" (Mt 26:34). Jesus could have simply said that Peter would deny him before dawn. Instead he tied Peter's awareness to sound rather than to sight. Suddenly the everyday, early morning sound of the crowing rooster became a soul-penetrating alarm. Peter's memory flashed back to their earlier exchange. He instinctively turned toward Jesus, and Luke tells us that "the Lord turned and looked straight at Peter" (Lk 22:61). The emerging dawn would never have sharpened Peter's painful awareness as did this single moment in time when he heard the sound of the rooster.

Up until this point we are not aware that Jesus and Peter were in visual range. How painful this moment must have been for Jesus. He was being spat upon, punched and slapped, but no blow had the force of Peter's denials (Mt 26:67). The early church found in Psalm 88 a sad description of this painful scene: "You have taken from me my closest friends and have made me repulsive to them. I am confined and cannot escape; my eyes are dim with grief" (Ps 88:8-9). Regardless of the intensity of the abuse he was suffering, Jesus heard the rooster and looked at Peter. We are told that Peter "went outside and wept bitterly" (Mt 26:75).

Years ago a friend of mine was arrested for drunk driving and spent a night in jail. To this day the sound of an iron gate clanging shut reminds him of that night when the jail door slammed behind him. Every time a dish breaks or a glass crashes, another friend of mine remembers the time she broke a dish belonging to her sister. She swept up the shattered pieces, buried them in the backyard and never told her sister. Thirty-five years passed before she admitted to her sister what she had done. Certain sounds can trigger the conscience, and this is exactly what happened to Peter. It is hard to imagine that Peter could ever forget the deeper meaning of that crowing rooster. Long after he had been forgiven, the sound of a rooster could recall this painful moment: the sound of his curse, the look in Jesus' eyes and the agony of soul. The abrasive sound of a crowing rooster cutting the predawn quiet was a powerful reminder.

I am amazed at how a terrible highway accident scene can often be returned to normal in an hour or so. Lanes blocked with smashed, overturned vehicles, injured drivers and passengers, fire trucks, highway patrol officers and ambulances are all quickly cleared, and traffic resumes. Passing motorists have no idea what transpired there a couple of hours earlier. I wonder how it would affect our driving if all the cars that were totaled in accidents were simply pushed to the side of the highway and allowed to remain as reminders. Maybe we should try that for a year and see if the visual impact of previous accidents lowers the accident rate. Jesus left Peter with a powerful reminder that I imagine he never forgot.

New Every Morning
But the crowing rooster reminded Peter of more than his denial of

Jesus. That is only half the story. The unmistakable sound of the rooster also reminded Peter of God's mercy and deliverance. For Peter, the crowing rooster signaled an end to willful self-rule and ego strength. Pride of self came to an abrupt end in bitter tears of personal repentance, and the night of denial gave way to the morning of deliverance. The sound of the rooster ended the night and heralded the light. It was fitting that some time later, after the resurrection, Jesus restored Peter by the Sea of Galilee in the morning. You recall that Jesus asked Peter three times, "Do you love me?" And Peter answered three times, "Yes, Lord, you know that I love you. . . . Lord, you know all things; you know that I love you" (Jn 21:15-17).

Later, when the apostle Peter emphasized the importance of the Word of God, he encouraged believers "to pay attention to it, as to a light shining in a dark place, until the day dawns and the morning star rises in your hearts" (2 Pet 1:19). Peter's reference to the morning star was a reference to his Lord and Savior, Jesus Christ (see Rev 2:28; 22:16), and now when Peter woke in the morning to the sound of a rooster, he was filled not with grief but with joy. As the psalmist said, "Weeping may remain for a night, but rejoicing comes in the morning" (Ps 30:5). "Satisfy us in the morning with your unfailing love, that we may sing for joy and be glad all our days" (Ps 90:14). No one knew better than Peter the truth of Lamentations 3:22-23: "Because of the LORD's great love we are not consumed, for his compassions never fail. They are new every morning; great is your faithfulness."

The rooster is a strange biblical image, but it was Jesus who drew it to Peter's attention and to ours for our own good. We were meant to hear the crowing rooster as a reminder to be watchful and vigilant. As Peter said, "Prepare your minds for action; be self-controlled; set your hope fully on the grace to be given you when Jesus Christ is revealed" (1 Pet 1:13). We were never meant to trust in ourselves or compare ourselves to others. The early morning crowing rooster was an effective daily reminder for Peter and the early church that each new day is to be lived in the presence and power of Jesus Christ. Peter's willful activism was slowly but surely transformed into willed passivity, and among the disciples he became an example of the discipline of surrender. If you don't live within the sound of a crowing rooster, maybe you should think about transferring the soul-triggering significance of the rooster's wakeup call to your alarm clock.

10

The Thorn
in the Flesh

To keep me from becoming conceited because of these surpassingly great
revelations, there was given me a thorn in my flesh,
a messenger of Satan, to torment me.
Three times I pleaded with the Lord to take it away from me.
But he said to me, "My grace is sufficient for you, for my power is made
perfect in weakness." Therefore I will boast all the more gladly about my
weaknesses, so that Christ's power may rest on me.
That is why, for Christ's sake, I delight in weaknesses, in insults,
in hardships, in persecutions, in difficulties.
For when I am weak, then I am strong.

2 CORINTHIANS 12:7-10

Even though the discipline of surrender is highlighted everywhere in
the Word of God, it is not easily embraced by us. We cling to the
notion that we minister out of our strength rather than our weakness.
Images of success dominate our understanding of self-worth, leadership, evangelistic effectiveness and church growth. We are tempted to
impose our standard of excellence rather than accept God's will of
sacrifice for the Christian life. God begins a good work in us, but in

no time we are suffering from an inflated ego. We are given to self-assertion to gain influence and self-promotion to gain respect. We're on the make, always competing for the upper hand, telling ourselves that this is how to relate to others and make a difference. We think it's our job to commend ourselves and project a positive self-image. *Or if we are not doing it ourselves, we are commending those who do!* We are well intentioned but fundamentally ignorant of how God works.

Maturity may be better measured in weakness than in strength, for only those who can truly say with the apostle, "I will boast all the more gladly about my weaknesses, so that Christ's power may rest on me" (2 Cor 12:9), have an understanding of how God works. Only those who have experienced real weakness appreciate the power of God's grace.

A Crown of Thorns

A dear friend of mine cannot look at a wreath without thinking of Christ's crown of thorns. The most festive Christmas wreath reminds her of the thorny crown thrust on her Savior's head. This emblem of suffering and pain recalls the deliberate mocking and intentional abuse that Jesus received at the hands of the Roman soldiers. After Pilate had feigned innocence and washed his hands of the whole affair, he had Jesus flogged and handed over to be crucified. The flogging alone would have drained every ounce of energy from his body. The Roman whip, made of leather straps embedded with small pieces of iron or bone, tore open his flesh. Barely able to stand, Jesus was paraded into the Praetorium before the entire company, which may have numbered up to six hundred soldiers. In a cruel and perverse way they used Jesus to entertain themselves. Whatever pent-up anger and animosity they felt toward the Jews could be vented on Jesus.

Pilate had asked Jesus directly, "Are you the king of the Jews?" and Jesus replied, "Yes, it is as you say" (Mt 27:11). It was this claim to sovereignty that the soldiers chose as their theme for mockery. They stripped Jesus of his outer garment, just as he himself had done when he washed his disciples' feet; and then they put a scarlet robe on him.

The blood from his back would have soaked through the robe. No one reading about this ordeal pictures stone-faced soldiers methodically robing and crowning Jesus. The Gospel accounts offer us the facts stripped of emotion. The Gospel writers write with restraint, not feeling the need to describe the obvious. But we can imagine Jesus center stage, enduring this mock coronation before a jeering audience. The crown of thorns is not placed gently on his brow but forced upon his head in mocking scorn.

Goaded by the raucous approval of their comrades, the soldiers had no thought for Jesus' humanity, let alone his deity. Having judged him a fraud and worthy of death, he was theirs to do with as they pleased. You can imagine the obscene gestures, the uncontrollable laughter and the cruelty on their faces as they repeatedly struck Jesus. Matthew tells us that they exclaimed, "Hail, King of the Jews!" as they spat on him and struck him with a staff "on the head again and again" (Mt 27:29-30). It is the crown of thorns that reminds us of this extreme humiliation. He wore this crown, which drew not only blood but also grief and sorrow. A crown of derision, not devotion, was driven down on his brow. But do we do more than witness this cruel coronation? Do we enter into his experience of humiliation and share this crown of pain even as we will someday wear a crown of glory?

There is a parallel between how the soldiers treated Jesus and how the world treats faithful Christians. This perspective is not intended to make Christians feel like victims but to prepare them for suffering. When Christians in a humble and Christlike way confess in word and deed that Jesus is the way, the truth and the life, scorn and ridicule are sure to follow. The Christian before the world is like Jesus before Pilate. He is our model of willed passivity, the picture of quiet dignity and unbending resolve that is meant to shape our praying imagination and impress us to the core. Our claim to knowing the truth seems as ludicrous to the world as Jesus' claim to be the King. Humanly speaking there is nothing about our confessions, commitments and convictions that the world finds convincing. In the light of our own strength, whether it be measured in status, wealth, education or popularity, we cannot hope to win the world.

More often than not the Christian looks silly to the world. Here we are, at the start of a new millennium, still believing in the incarnate One when the world tells us to believe in ourselves; still trusting the Savior when the world trusts in subjective feelings and secular science; still worshiping the Triune God, Father, Son and Holy Spirit— while the world worships money, sex and power. Should we be surprised that the way of the cross looks indefensible to the world? What the soldiers did to Jesus is what a world turned away from God does to the Christian. Jesus was of no significance to the soldiers, and they totally dehumanized him.

In thinking about how foolish Christians look to the world, I am reminded of John Sung, one of China's famous twentieth-century evangelists. After he completed a Ph.D. in chemistry from Ohio State University, Sung decided to study religion at Union Theological Seminary in New York before returning to China. What he found at Union Seminary confused him. Many of his professors denied the deity of Christ, preferring to present Jesus as an ideal to imitate rather than as the Savior of the world. They discounted biblical miracles, challenged the authority of the Word of God and promoted the social gospel. While at seminary Sung began to study Buddhism and Taoism, but nothing he studied satisfied. After years of pursuing science and religion he felt empty, and his sense of disillusionment and desperation grew. A popular, outgoing student leader at Ohio State, Sung became withdrawn and sullen at Union Seminary. He cut classes and kept to himself. His spiritual struggle climaxed one evening in February, when he became overwhelmed with a sense of his own sinfulness. He rummaged through his trunk for his New Testament, which he hadn't read in months, and turned to the story of the cross in Luke 23. There he saw in vivid detail, as if for the first time, the Savior who died for his sins. The sight of Jesus was so real to him that he felt as if he was at the foot of the cross. His prayers of repentance were answered with a powerful assurance of forgiveness. Sung became convinced that on that night God said to him, "Son, your sins are forgiven." Later, he would compare his experience to that of the apostle Paul on the Damascus road. The next morning he woke as a new man with a heartfelt desire to share the gospel. Union Theological Seminary hadn't seemed very concerned about John Sung as long as he was irritable, depressed and withdrawn. But after he emerged from his spiritual crisis with peace and joy, the administration arranged for a psychiatric examination and had him admitted to a sanatorium. "There is nothing wrong with my head!" he protested. "The trouble has been in my heart, but that is all right now!"[1] It probably didn't help that he set fire to some of his liberal theology books and stopped attending lectures.

For the next six months Sung made the mental hospital his theological college. He studied the Bible from cover to cover and prayed. He claimed that it was there that God taught him the difficult lesson of surrender to the will of God. In a psychiatric ward God dealt with Sung's bad temper and raised up an evangelist who would come to be known as the Wesley of China. As far as Sung was concerned his real seminary graduation occurred on August 30, 1927, the day he was discharged from the mental hospital, because that is where the Lord had met him in such a profound and life-changing way. The words of Isaac Watts's hymn express Sung's conviction:

> Forbid it, Lord, that I should boast,
> Save in the death of Christ, my God;
> All the vain things that charm me most—
> I sacrifice them to His blood.[2]

The Sign of the Cross

A remarkable pattern can be seen among the people God uses for his glory. They understand their weakness and learn to depend on God's strength. The life of Job illustrates the truth that runs through the Bible: "When I am weak, then I am strong" (2 Cor 12:10). Jacob's unusual encounter with God left him with a limp. Joseph was reduced to slavery. Moses felt he couldn't speak. The Israelites were vastly outnumbered when they entered the Promised Land. David's great-grandmother Ruth was, for a time, a poor widow. Hannah was barren until God heard her cry. Jeremiah was an object lesson of weakness; for forty years he stood outside the system calling people to God, without success. Daniel had no defense against political power plays other than God. Exiled in Babylon, Nehemiah was more than a thousand miles from where he wanted to serve God. Esther belonged to an endangered minority and risked her life for the sake of God's people. Amos and Micah had no credentials other than the fact that God called them to proclaim his word. John the Baptist was but a voice in the wilderness and the disciples of Jesus realized their weaknesses before they were useful in the kingdom of God.

We don't automatically come to the place where we boast of the things that show our weakness (2 Cor 11:30). But as we examine the biblical pattern, we do well to ask, "What has God allowed in my life to remind me of my weakness?" Self-commendation is so deeply ingrained within us that we need the vivid reminder of the crown of thorns. The apostle Paul clearly saw a connection between Christ's suffering and his own. He wrote, "I fill up in my flesh what is still lacking in regard to Christ's afflictions, for the sake of his body, which is the church" (Col 1:24). Paul didn't mean to imply that his suffering added in any way to the finished work of Christ, but he knew that to follow Christ was to participate in the suffering of Christ. Like our Lord Jesus, we stand before the Pilates of the world in weakness affirming a truth they neither understand nor appreciate. As Paul said, "the sufferings of Christ flow over into our lives" (2 Cor 1:5).

A Single Thorn

Paul's thorn in the flesh metaphor was especially well chosen for several reasons. First, not only does Paul's thorn in the flesh recall Christ's crown of thorns, but it draws a comparison that is both humble and true. Paul's suffering compared to Christ's suffering was as a single thorn compared to a wreath of thorns. Proportionately, Paul knew that his suffering could never compare to his Lord's suffering.

Second, the metaphor of a thorn is apt because it reminds us of Adam's fall. God cursed the ground because of human sin: "Cursed is the ground because of you; through painful toil you will eat of it all the days of your life. It will produce thorns and thistles for you" (Gen 3:17-18). It is especially noteworthy that Christ, who bore the entire burden of the Fall for us, should have been forced to wear a crown of thorns. And it is equally fitting that Paul recalled his own weakness and frailty through the symbol of a thorn. Third, as God permitted the Lord of glory to wear a crown of thorns, God permitted Paul, his apostle, to experience the constant, nagging reminder of his own weakness for the sake of God's glory.

The challenge Paul faced at Corinth was the criticism that he did not measure up to the so-called super-apostles. These rival teachers claimed to possess special wisdom (2 Cor 1:12) and bolstered their status by demanding high fees (2 Cor 2:17; 11:7). They promoted themselves (2 Cor 4:5) and projected an image of success (2 Cor 10:10). Paul was placed in the awkward position of defending himself. "I do not think I am in the least inferior to those 'super-apostles,' " Paul argued. "I may not be a trained speaker, but I do have knowledge" (2 Cor 11:5-6). Instead of responding to the humility and sacrifice that Paul and his team had repeatedly demonstrated, some of the believers were taken in by the super-apostles. The irony was not lost on Paul. "In fact, you even put up with anyone who enslaves you or exploits you or takes advantage of you or pushes himself forward or slaps you in the face. To my shame I admit that we were too weak for that!" (2 Cor 11:20-21).

Paul refused to stoop to self-commendation. Yes, he had the religious pedigree and the ecstatic experiences to boast about if he wanted to, but he preferred to talk about his weaknesses. "If I must boast, I will boast of the things that show my weakness" (2 Cor 11:30). He shared how he won the battle over self-promotion and self-preoccupation. Fourteen years before, he had a wonderful, powerful spiritual experience. He recounted his story in the third person, but he refused to go into the details. What was important, Paul insisted, was that because of "these surpassingly great revelations" he was given a thorn in his flesh, "a messenger of Satan," to torment him. The purpose of the thorn was "to keep [him] from becoming conceited" (2 Cor 12:7).

The application of the "thorn in the flesh" metaphor to our own lives is obvious. What has God placed in our lives to remind us of our weakness and Christ's power? As you might expect, there's considerable speculation about Paul's thorn in the flesh. Suggestions include eye inflammation, malaria and a speech impediment, on the physical side, and his pagan and religious opponents, on the spiritual side. Paul's reference to the flesh would seemingly indicate that it was a physical problem of some sort. No one knows for sure, but the range of possibilities suggests the variety of "thorns" the Lord could also use in our lives "to keep [us] from becoming conceited."

Is it coincidental that many of the believers we know who feel Christ's power resting on them willingly cope with evident weaknesses? And those who are sterile spiritually seem to be preoccupied with their self-importance. It is manifestly true that those who have accepted their weaknesses and turned to God are much easier to live with in the body of Christ than those who seek to impress us with their strengths.

Paul said that he pleaded with the Lord three times to take "it" away from him. This reminds us of Jesus in Gethsemane pleading with the Father three times, "If it is possible, may this cup be taken from me. Yet not as I will, but as you will" (Mt 26:39). God's answer to Paul cannot be categorized as negative. It is far more positive than Paul may have imagined at the time, because he was now empowered by the power of God.

I associate "My grace is sufficient for you, for my power is made perfect in weakness" (2 Cor 12:9) with a particular incident that took place when I was teaching in Taiwan. The occasion was not very profound, but it made a lasting impression on my soul. I had spent the entire night retching from food poisoning. In the morning I was to teach a class of fifty Chinese students on the subject of a Christian worldview. Many of the students were Buddhist, Taoist or animist, and I felt that the next day's lecture was especially important. The thought crossed my feverish mind: *Lord, why did you allow this tonight? This is very bad timing.* There was no one at the school to take my place, and I didn't want to cancel the class. In the morning I was totally exhausted, but at least my digestive system wasn't in major revolt. As I showered and got ready, I felt the Lord gave me this verse: "My grace is sufficient for you, for my power is made perfect in weakness." I went to the classroom and taught one of the best classes I had all year. I felt weak, but to my amazement it went well. Maybe the students were especially attentive because I looked half dead, but in any case I was encouraged and thankful to the Lord.

We miss Paul's point entirely if we play the role of victim. The thorn is not there to make us feel sorry for ourselves and seek the sympathy of other believers. The thorn is not an obstacle to God's will but a catalyst for doing God's will. A thorn doesn't put us on the disabled list. On the contrary, it prepares us for ministry. Weakness is not an impediment but a prerequisite for God's work. Paul lived his life this way. He wrote, "For Christ's sake, I delight in weaknesses, in insults, in hardships, in persecutions, in difficulties. For when I am weak, then I am strong" (2 Cor 12:10).

I believe that Paul's thorn in the flesh reminded him of Christ's crown of thorns. Whenever he was tempted to boast of his strengths, he remembered Christ's weakness. "For to be sure," Paul concluded, "he was crucified in weakness, yet he lives by God's power. Likewise, we are weak in him, yet by God's power we will live with him to serve you" (2 Cor 13:4).

John Milton, the great English poet, became blind in 1652. He may have thought his writing days were over. They were not. He went on to write his great epic poem, *Paradise Lost*, some twenty years later. But at the age of forty-four he came to terms with his weakness and learned the valuable lesson that God desires our faithfulness, not our achievements; our communion, not our conceit. A reader can recognize the power of Christ resting on Milton as he penned his famous sonnet in the year of his blindness:

When I consider how my light is spent,
Ere half my days, in this dark world and wide,
And that one Talent which is death to hide,
Lodg'd with me useless, though my Soul more bent
To serve therewith my Maker, and present
My true account, lest he returning chide;
"Doth God exact day-labor, light denied,"
I fondly ask; But patience to prevent
That murmur, soon replies, "God doth not need
Either man's work or his own gifts; who best
Bear his mild yoke, they serve him best; his State
Is Kingly. Thousands at his bidding speed
And post o'er Land and Ocean without rest:
They also serve who only stand and wait."
(John Milton, Sonnet XIX)

11

The Lamb of God

Surely he took up our infirmities and carried our sorrows,
yet we considered him stricken by God, smitten by him, and afflicted.
But he was pierced for our transgressions,
he was crushed for our iniquities; the punishment that brought us peace
was upon him, and by his wounds we are healed.
We all, like sheep, have gone astray, each of us has turned to his own way;
and the LORD has laid on him the iniquity of us all.
He was oppressed and afflicted, yet he did not open his mouth;
he was led like a lamb to the slaughter,
and as a sheep before her shearers is silent, so he did not open his mouth.
By oppression and judgment he was taken away.

ISAIAH 53:4-8

The next day John saw Jesus coming toward him and said,
"Look, the Lamb of God, who takes away the sin of the world!
This is the one I meant when I said,
'A man who comes after me has surpassed me because he was before me.' "

JOHN 1:29-30

For the Christian the life of surrender begins with an image of total surrender. Unless we depend on the sacrifice of Christ for our salvation, we have nothing to surrender. We have no life to give. As Jesus said, "I tell you the truth, unless you eat the flesh of the Son of Man and drink his blood, you have no life in you. Whoever eats my flesh and drinks my blood has eternal life" (Jn 6:53-54).

Peter's crowing rooster may be the most hidden biblical image we will explore. Its spiritual significance is passed over so quickly that we can easily miss it, but Jesus as the Lamb of God impresses almost everyone as an important religious symbol. The image of the Lamb brings to mind Psalm 23:1-2: "The LORD is my shepherd, I shall not be in want. He makes me lie down in green pastures, he leads me beside quiet waters." Our first thought is to apply this pastoral imagery to ourselves. "We are his people, the sheep of his pasture" (Ps 100:3). This gentle pastoral imagery conveys the positive idea of guidance, protection and provision. For many the symbol of the lamb may end there. It doesn't seem to work to present Jesus, whom we think of as the Good Shepherd (Jn 10), as the Lamb of God. But we need to take this biblical image further, where we have to be discerning, for the biblical imagery reflects both pastoral care and the passion of Christ. Jesus, the Good Shepherd, is the one and only sacrifice for our sins. We were meant to picture not only sheep by a quiet stream but a slain lamb on an altar of sacrifice.

The first part of this image seems familiar. It is comforting and easily associated with our felt needs. But for many the second part is foreign and strange, especially for modern people who have never seen an animal sacrifice. It would be very dramatic if we witnessed a real demonstration. What would happen if we actually sacrificed a lamb on an altar at church, and the sanctuary filled with the smoke and smell of a burnt sacrifice? I imagine some people would hastily leave, visibly upset. There would be considerable fallout from such an object lesson. Animal rights groups would protest, and the local newspaper would run the story on the front page. Readers would conclude that the church must be part of a strange cult. Religious rituals no longer include the sights and smells of slaughtered animals.

The Sacrifice

"Look, the Lamb of God, who takes away the sin of the world!" (Jn 1:29).

The imagery of the lamb goes back to the beginning, when God chose Abel's sacrifice of a lamb over Cain's offering of produce. Without explanation, God declared what was acceptable and let the imagery of the sacrificial lamb speak for itself. Noah and Abraham followed Abel's example and worshiped God with burnt sacrifices. When God told Abraham to go to a mountain in Moriah and sacrifice Isaac, Abraham obeyed (Gen 22:1-19). For three long, soul-searching days en route to the remote site, Abraham tried to understand the mind of God. Why was a sacrificial lamb unacceptable and an only son required? It was Isaac who asked the innocent, obvious question, "But where is the lamb for the burnt offering?" Abraham answered, "God himself will provide the lamb for the burnt offering, my son" (Gen 22:7-8). And sure enough, at the last moment God provided a lamb, and Abraham removed Isaac from the altar. Abraham had proved that he would not allow God's blessing of his only son, Isaac, to become a substitute for God himself.

God meant for this whole episode to go well beyond the ancient patriarch and his son. When Abraham said, "God himself will provide the lamb," he spoke far better than he knew. His willingness to sacrifice his one and only son became a picture of what God would do for us. "For God so loved the world that he gave his one and only Son, that whoever believes in him shall not perish but have eternal life" (Jn 3:16). The blood of the lamb became more vivid for the children of Abraham with the celebration of the Passover. To protect their first-born sons from the tenth plague, the Israelites were to kill a year-old male lamb without defect and sprinkle the blood on the doorframes of their homes. They were to eat the Passover meal in haste, ready for the exodus. The word of the Lord is shocking to modern ears:

> On that same night I will pass through Egypt and strike down every firstborn—both men and animals—and I will bring judgment on all

the gods of Egypt. I am the LORD. The blood will be a sign for you on the houses where you are; and when I see the blood, I will pass over you. No destructive plague will touch you when I strike Egypt. (Ex 12:12-13)

To this day the Passover is celebrated annually by orthodox Jews. Beginning with Aaron, the high priest, and the institution of the Day of Atonement, Israel was reminded of its need for forgiveness through an atoning sacrifice (Lev 23:26-32). Once a year the high priest entered the holy of holies and sprinkled the blood of a young bull that had been sacrificed to atone for the sins of the priest and his family. The blood that was shed for the sake of the high priest symbolically came between Aaron and the holy presence of God. Not only did Aaron's access to this inner sanctum depend on it, but so did his very life. Then Aaron slaughtered one of two specially designated goats for the sin offering of the people. The sacrifice was for "the whole community of Israel" because "of the uncleanness and rebellion of the Israelites, whatever their sins have been"(Lev 16:16-17). The other goat became the "scapegoat." Aaron laid his hands on the head of the goat and confessed "over it all the wickedness and rebellion of the Israelites—all their sins" (Lev 16:21). This goat was then released into the desert, symbolizing the removal of all sins from the community.

To many today this sounds superstitious and strange. But for the people of God, both then and now, it is a profound object lesson, a redemptive analogy. The Day of Atonement is a parable, reminding everyone of God's holy purity and our need for repentance and forgiveness. God kept making his point: "Without the shedding of blood there is no forgiveness" (Heb 9:22). The blood of lambs, bulls and goats did not take away sins, but the sacrifices pointed to the One who would and did. The Passover and the Day of Atonement foreshadowed the cross. Aaron was the precursor of our great High Priest, and the sacrifices pointed to the "once for all" sacrifice of Jesus Christ (Heb 10:10).

This is what John the Baptist had in mind when he introduced Jesus, declaring, "Look, the Lamb of God, who takes away the sin of the world!" (Jn 1:29). He wasn't evoking the pastoral image of sheep grazing in a field but the sacrificial lamb. Of all the things he might have said, this description was the most shocking and extreme. No one had ever implied that the Messiah, the Anointed One, was to fulfill the meaning of the sacrificial system. Up until John's introduction of Jesus this connection had never been drawn.

The prophet Isaiah wrote, "We all, like sheep, have gone astray, each of us has turned to his own way; and the LORD has laid on him the iniquity of us all." But no one had ever associated the description of the Suffering Servant, who "was led like a lamb to the slaughter," with the Anointed One—the Christ (Is 53:6-7). People would have expected the Messiah's forerunner to say, "Look, the conquering King, who comes to rule and reign!" Instead John proclaimed him the Lamb of God "who takes away the sin of the world" (Jn 1:29).

Far from distancing himself from the Old Testament sacrificial system and the need for atonement, Jesus emphasized that he had come to fulfill all that these sacrifices had been pointing to all along. "For even the Son of Man did not come to be served, but to serve, and to give his life as a ransom for many" (Mk 10:45). This is why Jesus took bread, gave thanks and broke it, and gave it to his disciples, saying, "This is my body given for you; do this in remembrance of me." And this is why he took the cup, saying, "This cup is the new covenant in my blood, which is poured out for you" (Lk 22:19-20).

Good by Nature, Naturally

The whole idea of animal sacrifices and slain lambs strikes moderns as cruel, barbaric and completely unnecessary. We would prefer to talk about self-esteem issues and eating disorders. We often see ourselves as victims of other people's sins, not our own. Poor parenting, inadequate education, bad luck, personal rejection, poverty, divorce, addictions and privations explain what's wrong with us. The problem with life is mitigating circumstances, not personal evil. Everyone and everything else is to blame except us and our sin. The fact that Jesus came to take away our sin and the sin of the world is not nearly as marketable as the notion that Jesus came to build up self-esteem or provide a sure-fire formula for success. There is no evidence that "Look, the Lamb of God" is turning any heads the way it did in Jesus' day. But the truth remains, "all have sinned and fall short of the glory of God" (Rom 3:23). The fact is "the wages of sin is death, but the gift of God is eternal life in Christ Jesus our Lord" (Rom 6:23).

Moderns are looking for a friendly Jesus who makes them feel better about themselves, but the biblical Jesus laid his life down that our sins might be forgiven. We are all better off when we realize that even the best of us are destined for hell apart from the atoning sacrifice of Christ. The true impact of the gospel has been felt only when people own up to their sin and turn to Christ for his forgiveness and redemption. They agree with the prophet Jeremiah, "The heart is deceitful above all things and beyond cure" (Jer 17:9). They echo the perspective of Isaiah, "All of us have become like one who is unclean, and all our righteous acts are like filthy rags; we all shrivel up like a leaf, and like the wind our sins sweep us away" (Is 64:6). If we were to use a medical term to describe our spiritual condition, we would say we're terminal. It's as if we all have full-blown AIDS or are filled with cancer. We cannot save ourselves; only God can save us.

The Blood of the Lamb

When we think of blood, most of us don't associate it with sacrifices. We identity blood with life. Bleeding is the surgeon's worst enemy. When an artery is cut, the doctor's first priority is to stop the bleeding. Dr. Paul Brand tells of a famous surgeon who used to ask his new students, "In case of massive bleeding, what is your most useful instrument?" Most young doctors guessed wrong. There was only one correct answer: "Your thumb, sir." Why? Dr. Brand explains, "The thumb is readily available—every doctor has one—and it offers a perfect blend of strong pressure and gentle compliancy."[1]

When I had surgery a number of years ago, I required six units of blood. There was a blood shortage at the time, and the doctors asked us if we knew people who would be willing to give blood. The need for blood was announced at the college faculty meeting where my father taught. Immediately six men left the meeting and went to the hospital to give blood. I don't think my father ever thought of their willingness to give blood for his son without choking up.

Modern medicine has made us aware of the preciousness of blood. Without it, we die. Every one of the one hundred trillion cells in our body needs the resources transported by blood. But as valuable as blood is to sustain physical life, the blood of the Lamb is infinitely more valuable. We are redeemed by "the precious blood of Christ, a lamb without blemish or defect" (1 Pet 1:19). Although we may shy away from the imagery of Christ's blood, the apostles embraced it as essential for understanding the cross and our salvation. Through "faith in his blood" we are able to draw near to the holy God (Rom 3:25; Eph 2:13). In Christ we are "justified" (Rom 5:9) and "redeemed" (Eph 1:7) and have "peace through his blood, shed on the cross" (Col 1:20). In the book of Revelation all praise is given "to him who loves us and has freed us from our sins by his blood" (Rev 1:5).

The apostles emphasized the cleansing power of Christ's blood. The blood of the Lamb cleanses our consciences (Heb 9:14) and "purifies us from all sin" (1 Jn 1:7). Those who are saved "have washed their robes and made them white in the blood of the Lamb" (Rev 7:14). Normally we think of blood as staining rather than cleansing. We scrub blood out; we don't wash with it. Yet the Bible is insistent on associating blood with cleansing, and Christian hymns celebrate it.

> What can wash away my sin?
> Nothing but the blood of Jesus. . . .
> Oh! precious is the flow
> That makes me white as snow;
> No other fount I know,
> Nothing but the blood of Jesus.[2]
>
> There is a fountain filled with blood
> Drawn from Immanuel's veins,
> And sinners plunged beneath that flood
> Lose all their guilty stains.[3]

It is remarkable that the theological meaning of blood corresponds so closely to the physiological use of blood. Biology helps to explain the theology of the cross. The circulatory system illuminates the sacrificial system. The role that blood plays in our bodies is absolutely astounding. Every cell in the body has to be tied into the capillary system if it is to survive. Individual red blood cells deliver oxygen through a chemical process of gas diffusion and transfusion and absorb waste products such as carbon dioxide and uric acid. These hazardous chemicals are then filtered out by the kidneys. The red blood cells are cleaned up and prepared for another payload of oxygen. Without blood constantly fueling the body with nutrients and cleansing our system of toxic chemicals, we couldn't survive. God chose an amazing analogy to illustrate our spiritual cleansing. The biblical symbolism of the blood of Jesus takes on fresh meaning for those who are familiar with modern medicine and unfamiliar with animal sacrifices. What blood does for the body, Christ's blood does for our souls.

The Lamb on the Throne

Flemish painter Jan van Eyck painted his *Adoration of the Lamb* in 1432. It can be seen today in the Cathedral of St. Bavon in Ghent, Belgium. It is a landscape, with cities and forests on the horizon and people groups in the foreground. Women and men, rich and poor, working class and scholars encircle an altar. The altar is in the center of the painting. There is a cross to one side and a column on the other side, symbolizing redemption and creation. Standing on the altar is a lamb, appearing healthy and strong, looking straight into our eyes. There is a hole in the chest of the lamb, and a stream of blood pours out, filling a chalice that stands on the altar.

Van Eyck's painting captures the biblical meaning of God's great gift of salvation. The Savior of the world is symbolically pictured as the Lamb that was slain, now standing in the center, encircled by angels and surrounded by people from every tribe and nation and language (Rev 5:6, 9). A fitting caption would be "Worthy is the Lamb, who was slain, to receive power and wealth and wisdom and strength and honor and glory and praise!" (Rev 5:12). It makes us want to stand and sing:

> Crown Him with many crowns,
> The Lamb upon His throne;
> Hark, how the heavenly anthem drowns
> All music but its own!
> Awake, my soul, and sing
> Of Him who died for thee,
> And hail Him as thy matchless King
> Through all eternity.[4]

The victory of the Lamb that was slain and the scene of universal adoration described in Revelation are powerful pictures of the consummation of God's work of salvation. But in keeping with our theme of the discipline of surrender, I would like to emphasize the humility of God, that he would use the imagery of the lamb to illustrate the extent of his love. Much of what has been said is to help us grasp the meaning and significance of this biblical image. Whether or not we find this symbol credible is important, but I find the humility of God infinitely more important. The greater mystery is that God would do this, not that we would accept this! The fact that the words of Isaiah apply to God is wonderful beyond description. "He was oppressed and afflicted, yet he did not open his mouth; he was led like a lamb to the slaughter, and as a sheep before her shearers is silent, so he did not open his mouth" (Is 53:7). There is no more powerful image of willed passivity than the Lord of glory, Creator of all and ruler of the cosmos, assuming the humility and submissiveness that remind us of a lamb, to cleanse our souls and make us whole.

> May the God of peace, who through the blood of the eternal covenant brought back from the dead our Lord Jesus, that great Shepherd of the sheep, equip you with everything good for doing his will, and may he work in us what is pleasing to him, through Jesus Christ, to whom be glory for ever and ever. Amen. (Heb 13:20-21)

12

The Empty Tomb

Early on the first day of the week, while it was still dark,
Mary Magdalene went to the tomb and saw that the stone had been
removed from the entrance. So she came running to Simon Peter
and the other disciple, the one Jesus loved, and said,
"They have taken the Lord out of the tomb,
and we don't know where they have put him!"
So Peter and the other disciple started for the tomb.
Both were running, but the other disciple outran Peter and reached
the tomb first. He bent over and looked in at the strips of linen lying there
but did not go in. Then Simon Peter, who was behind him,
arrived and went into the tomb. He saw the strips of linen lying there,
as well as the burial cloth that had been around Jesus' head.
The cloth was folded up by itself, separate from the linen.
Finally the other disciple, who had reached the tomb first, also went
inside. He saw and believed.

JOHN 20:1-8

Simple symbols like the unadorned altar and the thorn in the flesh,
the manna in the wilderness and the Lamb of God invoke powerful
spiritual truths about what it means to live in the will of God. The
images define for us in practical terms what it means to surrender our
lives to Christ. They capture the wisdom, character and passion of

taking up our cross daily and following Jesus. We respond to visual images because they help us handle concepts that might otherwise remain abstract and theoretical. Like a child's flannel-graph lesson they help to identify and visualize the truth of God.

All that we have come to understand about biblical images depends on the reality of the resurrection. If the bodily resurrection of Christ is a myth, then submitting to Jesus as Lord is a religious theory without merit. The resurrection is absolutely critical to our understanding of the relationship between the visible and the invisible. Apart from the reality of the risen Lord, we are left with empty symbols and meaningless images. The *empty* tomb is filled with meaning. The risen Lord Jesus infuses the symbols of the faith with meaning for us not only in time but for eternity.

Eye Contact

When we communicate, we like to make eye contact. I find it difficult to talk about something significant with people wearing sunglasses because I can't read their eyes. Phone calls are just not as good as face-to-face conversations because we can't see how a person is responding. Biblical images are important because they help us make eye contact with the truth. They give us a mental picture that enables us to visualize God's expectations.

We have explored biblical symbols, as opposed to works of religious art. Biblical images are rich in meaning, but they remain humble and earthy in appearance. They resist the human temptation to turn images into idols. We do not worship them as sacred objects; they are symbols not shrines. Their value is instructional, and their purpose is pedagogical. They are like the professor's diagrams on the chalkboard, hastily drawn to illustrate a concept. We might think of biblical images as *shorthand* notations for divine revelation. These illustrations are defined by the biblical text even as they illuminate biblical truth. Without biblical revelation giving each image context and content, they have no true meaning.

The power of the metaphor lies in its ability to illustrate rather than substitute for reality. This distinction is very important because we are strongly inclined, particularly in modern culture, to reduce reality to only what we can see. What we do not see, we judge to be unreal. It is important for us to understand that biblical images help us make eye contact with the real truth that can be seen only through the eyes of faith.

Clinging to Symbols

The women who went to the tomb on that first Easter Sunday morning are a picture of those who are sincere and sensitive but who have yet to become aware of the truth of the risen Lord. Mary of Magdala saw that the stone had been removed from the entrance to the tomb. "They have taken the Lord out of the tomb," she exclaimed, "and we don't know where they have put him!" (Jn 20:2). By bringing spices to anoint the body, the women were fulfilling a prescribed ritual for honoring a deceased loved one. Religious and cultural traditions can be helpful in getting us through difficult times, such as the loss of a family member. They give the living a way to express their grief, deal with their pain and help bring closure. According to custom the tomb was to become a memorial, a place to go to remember their times with Jesus.

On several occasions when I lived in Taiwan, I awoke early in the morning to the sound of a funeral procession. The mourners made their way through the village wailing and banging on metal drums to ward off evil spirits. The funeral vigil could go on for days in front of their small ramshackle dwellings, often accompanied by the burning of paper money and papier-mâché miniature homes, with the hope that these would materialize in the next life for the deceased. The ritual is a cultural way of dealing with death and grief.

As a pastor of an old mainline church, I meet people who cling to the symbols of the Christian faith, especially in weddings and funerals, but who have never experienced the power of the risen Lord. They come to church on Easter Sunday the way Mary of Magdala came to the tomb on Easter morning, because it is the traditional thing to do. Their motives are sincere, and they seek some spiritual comfort in these religious symbols, but it is difficult for them to distinguish between nostalgia and faith.

Like many other old downtown churches, we've had our share of religious funerals, like the one recently conducted for a young police officer killed in a car crash. He never attended our church, but his parents were married in the church thirty-five years ago. Their son's death brought them back to church for the funeral. More than a thousand officers attended to honor one of their own. Armed SWAT team officers were on the roof of the church, and hundreds of patrol cars were lined up outside for the procession to the cemetery. Among the platitudes intoned in King James English by the chaplain, there was only a passing reference to the resurrection, yet everything was done in the name of Christ. Christian symbols were featured in the ritual, but what did they stand for?

Jaroslav Pelikan has observed, "Tradition is the living faith of the dead; traditionalism is the dead faith of the living."[1] It is obvious that "the faith that was once for all entrusted to the saints" (Jude 3) has taken a backseat to traditionalism. I am reminded of Søren Kierkegaard's cryptic line, "Everything goes on as usual, and yet there is no longer any one who believes in it."[2]

The traditional church feels like a museum, the contemporary church like a stadium, and both can seem intent on manipulating Christian symbols in favor of the audience. Going to church on Easter may help a lot of people stay in touch with their roots and lift their spirits, but it doesn't help their relationship with the risen Lord. All too often the powerful symbols of the cross and the Eucharist are blended with an Easter egg hunt and the Easter bunny.

Religion that becomes all metaphor and symbol amounts to idolatry. It consists of external rituals, liturgies and religious performances, but without God. It doesn't matter whether it's Gregorian chants or Maranatha songs of praise, a Gothic cathedral or a school auditorium, the medium of worship becomes the object of worship, and knowing God is forgotten. Religion is dangerous for this very reason.

Religious styles and tastes, personalities and traditions have a way of becoming objects of devotion that distance sincere people from the very presence of the holy God they claim to worship. Instead of biblical images instructing believers in the discipline of surrender, cultural icons impose on unsuspecting religious people subtle forms of idolatry. The tomb is an appropriate symbol for such religion. It is dead.

Until there is a personal experience with the risen Lord Jesus, people will cling to religious symbols the way the Israelites bowed before the golden calf. Invariably the human heart pulls in something visible to stand in place of the living God. It may be money, sex or power, or it may be singing in the choir, preaching sermons or going on mission trips.

Standing beside the empty tomb, crying, Mary was sure that Jesus' body had been manhandled and carried away. Thinking that a person standing nearby was the gardener, she said, "Sir, if you have carried him away, tell me where you have put him, and I will get him" (Jn 20:15). She was willing to do whatever it took to show her love, to honor the memory of Jesus. But it was Jesus who stood outside the tomb and outside Mary's realm of understanding. He said to her, "Mary" (Jn 20:16). A single word and split-second recognition moved Mary from honoring a tradition to embracing her Lord. The resurrection of Jesus makes a personal relationship with the holy God possible. Mary goes from holding onto a memory to worshiping her Lord, from performing a ritual to following her Lord. Instead of an embalmed body encased in a tomb, Mary knows the risen Lord Jesus, exalted and soon to be ascended.

More Than Metaphor

Mary began Easter Sunday morning by clinging to tradition as the last vestige of her relationship to Jesus, and Thomas began the day by rejecting it. Like many today Thomas had no interest in manipulating the symbols and following the rituals. As far as he was concerned, it was over. He insisted on a real resurrection or nothing at all. There would be no middle ground for Thomas. Can we blame him for his skepticism? He had no interest in Jesus as a memory or Jesus as a metaphor. As far as he was concerned, his experience with Jesus was a closed book. That phase of his life was over. He would have nothing to do with wishful thinking and the religious imagination. He issued a challenge: "Unless I see the nail marks in his hands and put my finger where the nails were, and put my hand into his side, I will not believe it" (Jn 20:25). Thomas issued his ultimatum. If Jesus did not personally confront him with an actual body, he would continue to reject any notion of resurrection. It was either a bodily resurrection or nothing at all.

Jesus was under no obligation to prove himself to Thomas, but he did. For the sake of Thomas and for future believers, Jesus accepted the challenge of doubt and confronted Thomas. "Put your finger here," he ordered. "See my hands. Reach out your hand and put it into my side. Stop doubting and believe" (Jn 20:27). Whether Thomas actually felt his side or touched his hand, we do not know, but Thomas immediately went far beyond a grudging acknowledgment of the resurrection by exclaiming, "My Lord and my God!" (Jn 20:28). Doubt resolved, Thomas freely worshiped. Jesus humbly met the terms of credibility set by Thomas, not only for Thomas but for us. He proved the historical reality of his resurrection, but more than that, he affirmed that a relationship with Thomas mattered to him.

Our faith in the risen Lord matters to God as well. Resurrection faith does not call for a sacrifice of our intellect, but it does call us to go beyond the limits of ordinary experience and conventional thinking. There is no purely historical or naturalistic explanation for the resurrection. It is due to an act of God that happened in history but did not happen in terms of historical causality.

The Christian faith has always insisted on a real resurrection. The crucified Messiah is the risen Lord. To divorce Jesus from the biblical testimony of the resurrection effectively annuls Christian faith and practice. The resurrection is the major premise of the early Christian faith. The fact that a small band of disciples turned the world upside down is attributed to the bodily resurrection of Jesus (Acts 17:2-7). If the bones of Jesus disintegrated in an ancient tomb, then following Jesus is a sad delusion. John Updike's Easter poem affirms this truth.

Make no mistake: if He rose at all
it was as His body;
if the cell's dissolution did not reverse,
    the molecules reknit, the amino
    acids rekindle,
the Church will fall.

It was not as the flowers,
each soft Spring recurrent;
it was not as his Spirit in the mouths
    and fuddled eyes of the eleven
    apostles; . . .

Let us not mock God with metaphor,
analogy, sidestepping transcendence;
making of the event a parable, a sign
    painted in the faded credulity of
    earlier ages:
let us walk through the door.

The stone is rolled back . . .[3]

At the University of Toronto, St. Michael's College, I had the unusual experience of studying theology under teachers who did not believe in the bodily resurrection of Jesus Christ. The dilemma facing some of my professors was how to remain faithful to certain modern ideas about history and nature and at the same time believe in the resurrection. Since they had concluded that Jesus' bodily resurrection was impossible, they sought to reinterpret the resurrection to fit their notions of fact and history. They embraced the resurrection as a metaphor for new life or a symbol for starting over. They waxed eloquent about the spirit of resurrection, even as they dismissed the fact of the resurrection. They argued that it is the spirit of Jesus that lives on in the memory of his followers.

At the university I found myself feeling like Thomas. It must be a real resurrection or nothing at all. I sided with the apostle Paul: "If

Christ has not been raised, our preaching is useless and so is [our] faith. . . . If only for this life we have hope in Christ, we are to be pitied more than all men" (1 Cor 15:14, 19). The gospel of Jesus Christ would never have been written apart from the bodily resurrection. The early Christians knew that Jesus as a symbol provided neither comfort nor conviction. Either the resurrection of Jesus was true or it was false. There was no middle ground for metaphor. In the words of Updike, "Let us not mock God with metaphor." Jesus is not a state of mind. He is the Lord of the universe. Make no mistake, it is a real, historical, down-to-earth, bodily resurrection that is accepted by faith. Christian faith has always insisted on a real resurrection, and it always will.

The explanation for the reality of the resurrection must be found in God and believed by faith. Shall we limit the Creator of all to our conventional thinking? Is the Author of life bound by the laws of nature? "By faith we understand that the universe was formed at God's command, so that what is seen was not made out of what was visible" (Heb 11:3). Christians believe that the visible world we inhabit is a testimony to the Lord God, Maker of heaven and earth. "The heavens declare the glory of God; the skies proclaim the work of his hands" (Ps 19:1). The requirement of faith becomes greater for those who come after Thomas. As Jesus said, "Blessed are those who have not seen and yet have believed" (Jn 20:29).

The Eyes of Faith
Among all the disciples John was the first to interpret the significance of the empty tomb. He outran Peter to the tomb, but it was Peter who went in first. He "saw the strips of linen lying there, as well as the burial cloth that had been around Jesus' head. The cloth was folded up by itself, separate from the linen" (Jn 20:6-7). Finally John went inside. Even though the disciples still did not understand from Scripture that Jesus had to rise from the dead, John went into the empty tomb, saw and believed (Jn 20:8). He was the first to realize that what Jesus had been saying all along was really true. "I am the resurrection

and the life. He who believes in me will live, even though he dies; and whoever lives and believes in me will never die" (Jn 11:25-26).

I am writing this on the day after the memorial service for Bob Goodwin. On Sunday mornings this physically frail, eighty-nine-year-old saint would greet me after the worship service by grasping my hand in both of his, joyfully exclaiming how wonderful it was to worship the Lord Jesus Christ. His face had a marvelous way of radiating his love for the Lord. He expressed the eagerness of a child and the maturity of a man of God. It is easy for me to picture Bob Goodwin as one of the disciples on the road to Emmaus, especially when they describe their reaction to Jesus' teaching. "Were not our hearts burning within us while he talked with us on the road and opened the Scriptures to us?" (Lk 24:32). It was almost as if you could see Bob Goodwin's faith in his eyes. Imagine how those two disciples looked when they returned to Jerusalem and said, "It is true! The Lord has risen!" (Lk 24:34). If I were Rembrandt, I would use the face of Bob Goodwin to capture that look of faith and joy.

The Christian faith is not a collection of religious symbols designed to give shape to spiritual feelings. Jesus is not an icon for better living or an inspiration for humanity. He's not a symbol for being spiritual. He's not a metaphor for hope or courage or innocent suffering or anything else people want to make him out to be. Jesus is the risen Lord! The value of the Christian faith is found not in symbols and traditions. These are never ends in themselves but pointers to the One who said, "I am the way and the truth and the life. No one comes to the Father except through me" (Jn 14:6).

The value of the Christian faith is found in a personal relationship with the living Lord. As the apostle Paul said, "I want to know Christ and the power of his resurrection and the fellowship of sharing in his sufferings, becoming like him in his death, and so, somehow, to attain to the resurrection from the dead" (Phil 3:10). Faith is the earnest expectation of sight. As the author of Hebrews wrote, "Now faith is being sure of what we hope for and certain of what we do not see"

(Heb 11:1). We look forward to that day when we shall see him "face to face" and experience the unimaginable glory of his presence; our faith will be turned to sight, and we will know fully, even as we are fully known (1 Cor 13:12).

13

Jars of Clay

Therefore, since through God's mercy we have this ministry,
we do not lose heart. Rather, we have renounced secret and shameful ways;
we do not use deception, nor do we distort the word of God.
On the contrary, by setting forth the truth plainly we commend ourselves
to every man's conscience in the sight of God. And even if our gospel is
veiled, it is veiled to those who are perishing. The god of this age has
blinded the minds of unbelievers, so that they cannot see the light
of the gospel of the glory of Christ, who is the image of God.
For we do not preach ourselves, but Jesus Christ as Lord,
and ourselves as your servants for Jesus' sake. For God, who said,
"Let light shine out of darkness," made his light shine in our hearts to give
us the light of the knowledge of the glory of God in the face of Christ.
But we have this treasure in jars of clay to show that this all-surpassing
power is from God and not from us. We are hard pressed on every side,
but not crushed; perplexed, but not in despair;
persecuted, but not abandoned; struck down, but not destroyed.
We always carry around in our body the death of Jesus,
so that the life of Jesus may also be revealed in our body.

2 CORINTHIANS 4:1-10

The biblical images we have explored paint a vivid picture of what it means to take up our cross daily and follow Jesus. One thing is certain: the portrait of the discipline of surrender is not a paint-by-number amateur work. There is no easy-to-follow formula or patented technique for understanding and internalizing the discipline of surrender. There is no spiritual shortcut to "getting the picture." A true composition emerges only through prayer and careful study of God's Word; anything less leaves us with an undeveloped, even distorted, picture of what is involved in submitting to the Lord Jesus.

Symbols of Surrender

Behind each of the symbols is a true story that leads us to the truth. The *unadorned altar* is a reminder not to turn our service and worship of God into an opportunity for self-expression and self-promotion. The simple *shepherd's staff* stands for the immediate presence and authority of God in our lives. *Manna in the wilderness* reminds us that only Jesus is the true Bread of Life. We cannot live apart from dependence on him. *Gideon's trumpet* announces that God's strategy of success has remained the same through the ages. The battle is the Lord's. We'll never succeed if we fight with the weapons of the world. Victory will always come " 'not by might nor by power, but by my Spirit,' says the LORD Almighty" (Zech 4:6).

Christ's invitation to take up the *easy yoke* offers a picture of partnership with Jesus. We lay aside the burdens that others and we pose upon ourselves, and we become committed to Christ and his agenda. The easy yoke is essential, not optional, if we expect to follow Jesus. The *towel and basin* signify the priority our Lord places on humble, ego-sacrificing service. The *borrowed donkey* reminds us to approach others with the gospel in humility and gentleness. Peter's *crowing rooster* is a spiritual wakeup call, a reminder to be watchful and vigilant. Our Lord calls us to account and holds us responsible for our confession and commitment. The apostle Paul's *thorn in the flesh* reminds us that Christ's grace is sufficient for us no matter what and that God's power is made perfect in our weakness.

There is no more powerful symbol for the discipline of surrender than the *Lamb of God*. It is a graphic metaphor depicting Christ's sacrifice on the cross for our salvation. If the Lord of glory humbled himself in this way to cleanse our souls and make us whole, how much more should we, who don't deserve his love, be willing to serve him humbly? The *empty tomb* points to the One who fills these symbols with true and lasting meaning, our risen Lord and Savior Jesus Christ.

We have studied these biblical symbols and tried to draw out their significance so that we can better visualize the life of faith. Biblical images were never intended to be ends in themselves. They are object lessons of instruction, not devotion, that lead us to greater fellowship and faithfulness with the living Lord Jesus. If we follow these images to their source, we find the true and living God, not a symbol. Jesus is not a symbol. He is not a metaphor for higher living or an icon for spiritual feelings. He is alive and invites us into a personal relationship with himself.

Symbols of Pride

The risen Lord Jesus is not a symbol, and those who follow Jesus are not symbols. Nevertheless there is considerable pressure to make others, as well as ourselves, into religious icons. Instead of being real in our relationship with the living Lord Jesus, we succumb to the subtle and not so subtle pressure to conform to religious expectations. Whether we foster this feeling or it is imposed on us, we attempt to maintain a certain image in order to be respected and held in high regard. We think we are doing the right thing by setting a positive example, maintaining religious morale and encouraging others to copy us. Most of us face this pressure to perform and to be something we're not for the sake of others. Sometimes we fake it to make it. This pressure impacts not only missionaries and pastors but parents, families and friends. Instead of Christ's call to obey, we act as though we have a religious role to play. Instead of being transformed by the renewing of our minds, we conform to people's expectations.

As we've seen, biblical images can shape our thinking in unexpected ways. They work like parables, engaging our minds and encouraging us to change the way we think and live. The Spirit of

God uses these object lessons to help us grasp truth that we would not otherwise understand. In contrast, religious icons tend to reflect personal opinions and cultural experiences. They only mirror back to us whatever thoughts and feelings they trigger within us. Religious symbols are a lot like patriotic symbols. The American flag or the queen of England may stir national pride in the same way stained glass windows and robed clergy may inspire spiritual feelings and loyalty to religious authority. Biblical images require biblical interpretation. The meaning and significance of the yoke, lamb, thorn and altar are derived solely from the Bible. Religious icons are subject to the observer's feelings, opinions and experiences. We can make religious symbols mean whatever we want them to. Interpretation is in the eye of the beholder, not in the text of God's Word. Religious icons can stir powerful sentiments. To many they represent authority and order and may inspire deep feelings of mystery and cultural pride. They give shape and expression to spiritual feelings, but they fail to articulate the truth of God's Word the way biblical images do. It is important to distinguish between religious icons and biblical images if we are to visualize the faith truthfully.

When a person receives the title *Reverend,* puts on a clerical robe, assumes an authoritative demeanor, speaks in an affected tone and anticipates people's respect, he or she may be aspiring to be a religious icon. Some pastors strive to become a symbol to their congregation. Depending on their tradition, robes and titles may or may not be important, but the ambition remains the same. For them the ministry is merited, a position for which they have been trained. And having graduated from seminary they feel qualified. Throughout their career the size and status of their congregations determine their rank and status. Their value lies not so much in what they say and do as in their presiding presence. They symbolize the church. They either embody its authority or personify its popularity, and sad to say, many congregations expect and encourage this mindset.

The temptation is great to turn a pastor into an idol. People make their pastor into a religious symbol because they would rather see what they believe than walk by faith. To some extent they imagine their pastor living out the faith for them. He studies the Bible to preach to them, so why should they study the Bible? He intercedes for them, so why should they pray? He officially witnesses and comforts, so why should they do it? And if the pastor challenges them to serve, they can always claim that they are not gifted to serve. In other words, the pastor is the minister, and they are the faithful and often admiring flock (audience).

On Sunday morning they experience faith vicariously through their pastor's experience. They know him better than they know Christ because he has made his personality and experience the focus of attention. They are spiritual dependents, having become so attached to their pastor's religious expression that they don't know how to pray, study the Bible, comfort others or witness. They have gone to church all of their lives, but they don't know how to live the faith. They don't know how to comfort family members in the hospital or speak of Christ to their neighbor. Sadly, they feel as dependent on the pastor for their spiritual welfare as they do on their doctor for medical advice.

The distinction between clergy and laity is deeply ingrained in religion and contradicts the description of believers we see throughout the Word of God. The prophets and apostles referred to their work in blue-collar ways. They colored their job description in earth tones. The prophet Ezekiel was a watchman (Ezek 33). John the Baptist was a voice in the wilderness (Jn 1:23). The apostle Paul's favorite self-designation was simply "a servant of Christ." The word he used literally meant "slave," but Paul's emphasis was not on servitude as much as privilege.[1] He was not humiliated by his calling; he was humbled by it. When Paul referred to himself and others as Christ's ambassadors, he was calling attention not to his status but to his responsibility (2 Cor 5:20). On the island of Patmos, the apostle John wrote a memorable description of himself: "I, John, your brother and companion in the suffering and kingdom and patient endurance that are ours in Jesus" (Rev 1:9). If the apostles didn't see themselves as symbols of the faith, occupying elite positions of religious authority, then neither should those today who consider themselves ministers of the gospel.

Many pastors who wear robes and preach from high pulpits are true signs of humility. To them the robes signify not status but submission to the Word of God. The pulpit is raised not to elevate their egos but to lift up the Word of God. Every time they put on their robes they pray that they will be faithful and obedient to the gospel of Christ. They are not a special class of believers who are a cut above the rest. A minister of the Word and sacrament is called to humble service in the name of Christ.

The biblical emphasis on the priesthood of believers strikes a blow against the distinction between clergy and laity and any notion of the ministry as a position of rank and status. The choice words and special titles are reserved exclusively for each and every believer. We are "a chosen people, a royal priesthood, a holy nation, a people belonging to God, that [we] may declare the praises of him who called [us] out of darkness into his wonderful light" (1 Pet 2:9).

But human nature is inclined to make icons out of saints, to set certain believers up on a pedestal and use them as symbols and authority figures to represent the ideal. There is a strong tendency to turn them into religious celebrities. Some people, by virtue of position, charisma, gifts and abilities, are deemed special and represent what others would like to become. Protestants don't think of ourselves as turning saints into icons, but we do it all the time. We don't paint them in Byzantine fashion with halos around their heads, but we use their smiling faces and well-crafted, public-relation images to promote religious work and inspire us. Whenever we build on a person's popularity or family name or capitalize on a particular saint's image, we are forgetting the apostle Paul's conviction: "We have this treasure in jars of clay to show that this all-surpassing power is from God and not from us" (2 Cor 4:7).

Clay Pots
The apostle Paul refuted the so-called super-apostles by conceding

that he was simply a *clay pot*. He chose this metaphor intentionally to highlight what for him was a most obvious truth: the issue was not his appearance or his eloquence or his popularity but the authority and power of the gospel of Jesus Christ (2 Cor 10:7-18). Paul chose a classic willed-passivity response. If aspiring religious icons sought to demean his ministry in order to enhance their status in the Corinthian church, so be it, but Paul wouldn't play their game. He had no desire to compete in the battle of the résumés (2 Cor 3:1-2). He compared his sufferings to their successes, his self-denial to their superiority, his weakness to their strengths. He could have lorded it over the Corinthians, but instead he worked with them for their joy (2 Cor 1:24). He could have peddled the word of God for profit, but instead he spoke as a man in Christ sent from God (2 Cor 2:17). He could have played the religious professional, but instead he surrendered his life that they might know Christ.

On a personal level Paul's strategy for demolishing "every pretension that sets itself up against the knowledge of God" can be summarized in an aptly chosen biblical symbol (2 Cor 10:5). Like the other biblical images we have examined, clay pots mean nothing aesthetically but something of significance biblically. A common, ordinary clay pot is just a clay pot. Paul wasn't referring to a Ming dynasty vase or a beautifully hand-painted bone china teapot. On the contrary, he saw himself as a plain vessel at God's disposal for the sake of the gospel. His letter to the Corinthians helps illustrate the difference between a biblical image and a religious icon.

Paul was the first to admit that he had received this ministry through the mercy of God. He refused to claim, as his opponents had, that he had gained the ministry through human merit. The difference between ministry based on the mercy of God and religious work based on human merit is the critical difference between calling people to Christ and selling people on religion. For Paul the issue was not what others thought of him but how they responded to Christ.

Paul also was committed to "setting forth the truth plainly." "We have renounced secret and shameful ways," he insisted. "We do not use deception, nor do we distort the word of God" (2 Cor 4:2-3). If people refused to accept the gospel, the reason could not be found in Paul's alleged lack of eloquence and rhetorical technique. It was because "the god of this age has blinded the minds of unbelievers, so that they cannot see the light of the gospel of the glory of Christ, who is the image of God" (2 Cor 4:4).

It was not Paul's purpose to impress people with himself. "We do not preach ourselves, but Jesus Christ as Lord, and ourselves as your servants for Jesus' sake" (2 Cor 4:5). For Paul it was important for people to know Christ, not the communicator. He had no desire for people to become dependent on his spirituality or attached to his personality. His aim was to encourage growth in Christ, not foster loyalty to himself.

Finally, Paul refused to project himself as an image of success. As in our own day, there were those who felt the sign of God's blessing was popularity, prosperity and prestige. The "super-apostles" promoted an image of excellence and success. They expected people to look up to them and revere them as symbols of divine blessing and endowment. The exact opposite was true in Paul's case. "We are hard pressed on every side, but not crushed; perplexed, but not in despair; persecuted, but not abandoned; struck down, but not destroyed" (2 Cor 4:8-9). All the biblical images that we have studied point to the sacrifice of the cross. Unlike religious icons that often point to human power and prestige, biblical symbols point to the way of the cross. Paul emphasized this point: "We always carry around in our body the death of Jesus, so that the life of Jesus may also be revealed in our body" (2 Cor 4:10). Paul freely admitted that he felt hemmed in, but not hammered; beat up, but not beaten; confused, but not confounded; knocked down, but not knocked out.

These were the reasons Paul gave for not losing heart in the ministry. The work we are called to do rests solely on mercy, not merit; integrity, not ingenuity. It rests on our Savior, not on ourselves; and on sacrifice, not success. Paul's clay pot metaphor is a fitting symbol for those who have surrendered themselves to Christ and echo in their souls John the Baptist's aphorism "He must increase, but I must decrease" (Jn 3:30 KJV). Instead of turning ministry into a battle of self-esteem, falling into the performance trap and promoting a public-relations image, Paul comfortably and confidently accepted the fact that "we have this treasure in jars of clay to show that this all-surpassing power is from God and not from us" (2 Cor 4:7).

Paul was not the first to use the jars of clay metaphor. The prophet Jeremiah introduces us to this object lesson. The Lord told him, "Go down to the potter's house, and there I will give you my message" (Jer 18:2). We have seen how often God employs visual aids to teach us the truth. So Jeremiah went down to the potter's house and observed him at his wheel. What impressed the prophet was the control that the potter had over the clay. As the potter rotated the wheel, he was able to shape the clay in whatever form he pleased. If the potter found some defect in the clay or it didn't conform to the potter's design, he could squeeze it into a lump and start over. The message for Jeremiah was clear: God is sovereign. The Lord has the power and the authority to shape his people according to his will. The question is this: How willing are we to be fashioned according to the will of God?

Biblical images are designed by God to guide us personally in what it means to follow our Lord Jesus. It is one thing to understand these images intellectually and another thing to be shaped by them. Does the unadorned altar change the way we worship? Are we moved by the Lamb of God, empowered by the thorn in the flesh and humbled by the borrowed donkey? Do we see ourselves under the yoke of Christ? Are we willing to use the towel and basin in humble service? Does the empty tomb fill us with the joy of the risen Lord? One thing is for sure: God has made his will known. If we don't get it, it's not because God has kept the discipline of surrender a mystery. He has illustrated his truth.

Notes

Chapter 1: Biblical Images
[1]Gerald F. Hawthorne, *Philippians*, Word Biblical Commentary (Waco, Tex.: Word, 1983), p. 75.

Chapter 4: Manna in the Wilderness
[1]Tom Wolfe, *A Man in Full* (New York: Farrar, Straus and Giroux, 1998), p. 292.
[2]Andrew Murray, *God's Best Secrets* (Grand Rapids, Mich.: Zondervan, 1979), p. 6.

Chapter 6: The Easy Yoke
[1]Jon Krakauer, *Into Thin Air* (New York: Anchor, 1997), p. 154.
[2]Max Lucado, "Max's Maxims," *Christianity Today*, February 8, 1999, p. 67.

Chapter 7: The Towel & Basin
[1]Simon Chan, *Spiritual Theology* (Downers Grove, Ill.: InterVarsity Press, 1998), p. 88.
[2]Robert Lowry, "Nothing but the Blood" (1876).
[3]As told by Steve Goodier, 1998.

Chapter 8: The Borrowed Donkey
[1]George Müller, *The Autobiography of George Müller* (New Kensington, Penn.: Whitaker, 1984), p. 73.
[2]Ibid., p. 80.

Chapter 9: The Crowing Rooster
[1]David W. Gill, *Peter the Rock: Extraordinary Insights from an Ordinary Man* (Downers Grove, Ill.: InterVarsity Press, 1986), p. 111.

Chapter 10: The Thorn in the Flesh
[1]Leslie T. Lyall, *John Sung: Flame for God in the Far East* (Chicago: Moody Press, 1964), p. 43.
[2]Isaac Watts, "When I Survey the Wondrous Cross" (1707).

Chapter 11: The Lamb of God
[1]Paul Brand and Philip Yancey, "Blood: The Miracle of Life," *Christianity Today*, March 4, 1983, p. 39.
[2]Robert Lowry, "Nothing but the Blood" (1876).
[3]William Cowper, "There Is a Fountain" (1771).

[4]Matthew Bridges, "Crown Him with Many Crowns" (1851), rev. Godfrey Thring (1874).

Chapter 12: The Empty Tomb

[1]Jaroslav Pelikan, *The Christian Tradition: A History of the Development of Doctrine* (Chicago: University of Chicago Press, 1971), 1:9.

[2]Søren Kierkegaard, "Either/Or: A Fragment of Life," in *A Kierkegaard Anthology*, ed. Robert Bretall (Princeton, N.J.: Princeton University Press, 1946), p. 81.

[3]Richard Lischer, " 'Resurrexit': Something to Preach," *Christian Century*, April 2, 1980, p. 372, quoting John Updike, *Telephone Poles and Other Poems* (New York: Knopf, 1963).

Chapter 13: Jars of Clay

[1]Ralph P. Martin, *2 Corinthians*, Word Biblical Commentary (Waco, Tex.: Word, 1986), p. 80.